BAT

The Absolute Guide

by
Neill Menneer & Kirsten Elliott

Published by
ktwo

In association with Find It Bath

Credits
Photography by Neill Menneer
Text by Kirsten Elliott
Line Illustrations by Grahame Baker-Smith
Design by Icehouse Design and Ktwo
Artwork Production by Jesse Loughborough, Ktwo
Edited by Neill Menneer

First published in 2004 by Ktwo,
Belgrave Lodge, Upper Camden Place, Bath BA1 5JA

© 2004 Neill Menneer. All rights reserved. No part of this publication may be reproduced or transmitted in any form by any means without prior permission from the publisher. ISBN 0-9542512-2-9

Introduction

Welcome to Bath, World Heritage Site & one of England's most beautiful cities.

From the beginning the town was blessed with a rare natural beauty. Its steep cliffs, to north and south, cradle a fertile valley through which the river Avon slowly snakes. In the heart of the town gushes its most spectacular and valuable asset, the Hot Springs. These thermal wonders produce over a million litres of mineral water every day and flow at a constant and luxurious 46 degrees celsius. From the dawn of time people have been attracted to their unique and magical properties leaving the town steeped in history from the Celt, Roman, Medieval and especially Georgian periods. Between 1714 and 1800 Bath found itself at the centre of the civilised world. The Beau Monde came to gamble, take the waters and strike a pose. The Picturesque Movement found its perfect setting here and Palladian architects made full use of the landscape's elegant lines and undulating hills. Despite this historical wealth and diversity Bath is actually a very small city (85,000 population) and can be crossed from North to South in less than an hour by foot. **We believe that no town in England rewards the walker quite like Bath.**

This book will guide you through the town by breaking it down into eight distinct areas. Each chapter deals with one section at a time and will provide you with an historical overview and facts about all the major buildings or sites to be found there. Each circular walk (one hour or less) has been especially created to maximise your enjoyment of the area and will lead you past, or to, the most important places of interest. The Sidetrack pages at the end of each chapter will ensure that you miss nothing of historical or aesthetic value. **If you like shopping or want to eat, drink or be merry we provide full listings at the back of the book.** This directory is thoroughly compiled and offers comprehensive up to date information on shops, cafes, restaurants, hotels and guesthouses. The icons indicate the specialism of each shop and help you find exactly what you're looking for. **We also provide further information and many other free resources on line at: www.finditbath.co.uk**

This booklet is a celebration of Bath's incredible heritage. In it you will find eight city walks, over 200 unique photos and 300 facts. Enthusiastically compiled by a team of local professionals who live and work in Bath, we wish to share our love and knowledge of the city with you.

Enjoy!

Neill Menneer, Publisher

Contents

Chapter 1	**The Royal Crescent**	**.4**
	The Royal Crescent	.8
	Cavendish Crescent	.10
	Somerset Place	.11
Chapter 2	**Lansdown Crescent**	**.16**
	Lansdown Crescent	.20
	Beckford's Tower	.22
Chapter 3	**Camden Crescent**	**.28**
	Camden Crescent	.32
	Walcot Street	.34
Chapter 4	**The Circus**	**.40**
	The Circus	.44
	Milsom Street	.46
	The Assembly Rooms	.47
Chapter 5	**Queen Square**	**.52**
	Queen Square	.56
	The Theatre Royal	.58
Chapter 6	**The Roman Baths**	**.64**
	The Roman Baths	.68
Chapter 7	**Bath Abbey**	**.78**
	Bath Abbey	.82
	The Guildhall	.84
Chapter 8	**Pulteney Bridge**	**.90**
	Pulteney Bridge	.94
	Sydney Gardens	.96
Chapter 9	**Widcombe Manor**	**.102**
Listings	**Shopping Highway**	**.114**
	Cafés & Fast Food	**.119**
	Guest Houses	**.121**
	Hotels	**.123**
	Museums	**.125**
	Galleries	**.126**
	Restaurants	**.126**
	Retailers	**.129**
	Things To Do	**.137**
	General Listing	**.139**
	Quiz & Trivia Pages	**.140**
	Map of Bath	**.142**

THE WALKS
How to use the Ktwo Maps

A few things to keep in mind when embarking on our walks:

1. The walks are circular. If you follow the walk we suggest, you will finish in the same area you started. We provide suggested starting points (**W**) but the walks may be started and finished at any point. And even crossed over and combined with walks from other chapters.

2. Deviation from the suggested walk is encouraged. The main walks are in green (— — —) but there are many alternative routes marked in red (·······). If you like structure when touring a new place, follow the green routes and you will see all the main features of Bath. The red routes are for those who like a little more freedom to explore, and will reveal more of Bath's character and hidden delights.

3. Each chapter has a Walk Overview box containing a list of the streets you will follow on the green part of the walk plus the main tourist sites along the way. Any letters or numbers in brackets in these boxes refer to the coloured circles on the maps.

4. On each chapter map you will see coloured icons, go to page 142 for a full map and a key. The numbers in white squares ([1]) are chapter-specific and refer to the numbered photos that appear at the end of each chapter.

The Royal Crescent
John Wood's Masterpiece

Chapter One

The Northwest

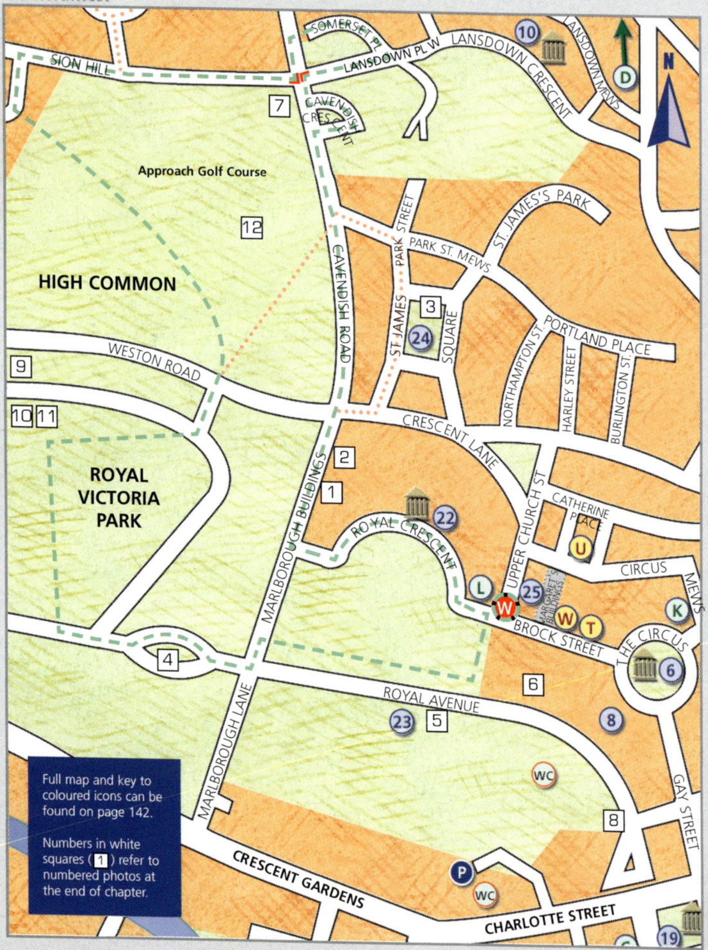

Chapter One - Introduction

Although Bath is known as a Georgian city, many of its most famous landmarks were not built until over halfway through the 18th century. Principal among these is the glorious sweep of Royal Crescent, designed by John Wood the Younger in 1766 and completed in the early 1770s. Standing proudly on a south-facing hillside, it was one of the first developments to enjoy the view over Crescent Fields. Here Jane Austen strolled in May 1801, although the weather was too cold for her to stay long. In 1830 the Royal Avenue was created as a carriage drive to the newly planted Royal Victoria Park, where today modern visitors enjoy the sports facilities or even take a ride in a hot-air balloon. North of the Crescent runs Julian Road, on the line of the Roman highway from Bristol, and north of that again lies St James's Square. This was built early in the 1790s on the site of an orchard, to the disgust of the Crescent's residents who preferred apple trees to new houses.

Looking out across the Approach Golf Course is Cavendish Place, a terrace which climbs sinuously up the hillside. Above it, by the same architect, John Pinch, is the severe quadrant of Cavendish Crescent. This contrasts vividly with the exuberant Somerset Place, designed by John Eveleigh. His buildings often cause great distress to purists, as he would cheerfully break the strict Palladian rules of architecture. Unfortunately he also sometimes ignored geology, and a combination of collapsing houses and collapsing finances caused him to leave Bath, from where he disappeared into obscurity. Perhaps he was unable to change to the new simple style popular in Regency times, unlike his contemporary Pinch.

This north-west corner of the city is certainly a place to linger. Whether your taste is for architecture, nature, or history, this area has it all.

WALK OVERVIEW:

Brock Street	Somerset Place
No. 1 Royal Crescent (L)	Sion Hill
Royal Crescent (22)	Footpath through High Common
Marlborough Buildings	**Royal Victoria Park (23)**
Cavendish Road	**Victoria Obelisk (4)**
Cavendish Crescent	Marlborough Buildings
Lansdown Place West	Footpath parallel to Royal Avenue

Chapter One

ROYAL CRESCENT

In 1766 John Wood the Younger took a lease on land from Sir Benet Garrard to build "good stone messuages in a workmanlike manner". Building began in 1767 and all the houses were occupied by 1778.

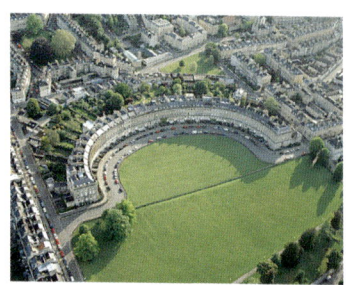

There are 30 houses in a crescent 164 metres across.

The facade is decorated with 114 giant order Ionic columns, i.e. the columns extend over two floors.

Some architects are critical of the centre. Usually there is a grand feature, but here John Wood the Younger simply marks it with two pairs of double columns, with a crescent-shaped window over the main window.

Only the façade was designed by John Wood. Individual builders then erected whatever they liked behind as long as they put the right bit of façade on the front.

No 1 was built first, to show the other builders what they were supposed to do.

Chapter One

Below the crescent there were fields where animals grazed. To keep them from coming too near the crescent a sunken wall was built. Horace Walpole says this was called a haha because the common people, not knowing about such a thing and finding the ground disappearing from their feet, would cry out "Ha! Ha!" in surprise.

The inventor of the modern shorthand, Sir Isaac Pitman, lived at No 17 in 1896.

Jane Austen visited the Crescent in June 1799 to watch Lady Willoughby "present the colours to some Corps of Yeomanry or other."

The Royal Crescent features in a scene in Charles Dickens's "Pickwick Papers". Mr Winkle locks himself out of his lodgings, hides in a sedan chair, and ends up being chased around the crescent.

Chapter One

CAVENDISH CRESCENT

Cavendish Crescent was originally called Winifred's Crescent. The area was once called St Winifred's Dale, the stream that ran beside it coming from St Winifred's Well. This rises in the grounds of what is now Bath Spa University College, higher up the hill.

The crescent was built between 1815 and 1829, the architect was John Pinch.

At the back of the crescent can be seen several of Bath's famous (or notorious) hanging loos. Added after the houses were built, they sometimes fell off, taking unwary occupants with them.

The crescent is one of the first to allow the servants in the garrets a view. The attic windows are in the front wall instead of being hidden behind a balustrade, as was normal.

Below the crescent is a house designed by Pinch in 1823. Constructed to look like one, it is in fact two houses.

Called Winifred's Dale, it is the only house that keeps the old name of the area. The post box on the corner is unusual because it has the cipher of Edward VII. Very few were made, since he only reigned for nine years.

Chapter One

SOMERSET PLACE

Somerset Place began as a pair of houses that today form the centre of the crescent. They are shown in a picture of 1792. The architect was John Eveleigh.

Work began to add the wings soon afterwards, but economic depression meant the houses were very slow to sell. Some were still unfinished in 1820. The west wing was never completed.

The centre is topped by a great broken pediment. This does not mean it needs repair, but that it does not join in the middle.

The two central houses have grotesque 'icicle carving' faces over each door. They are said to have been added as a reminder of the terrible winters of the 1790s.

The Crescent is now part of Bath Spa University.

Chapter One - The Walk

THE WALK
Places to discover on the Chapter One Walk

Marlborough Buildings (1 & 2), to the west of the Royal Crescent, was built around 1790.

In 1791 the Duke and Duchess of Devonshire took one house in Marlborough Buildings for themselves and their servants and another for their small son and his servants. No tradesman was permitted to call at the son's house for fear of introducing smallpox.

The architect of **St. James's Square** (3) was John Palmer. A plan of 1786 shows land belonging to Sir Peters River Gay, with a design for a square sketched on it.

The residents of the Royal Crescent who had gardens and orchards here were very upset. Christopher Anstey wrote a satirical poem to express his indignation.

A plaque on No. 35 says Charles Dickens stayed here. In fact, it was his friend Walter Savage Landor who lived here. Dickens just came for dinner one evening.

Chapter One - The Walk

Park Street, which leads out of the square, is also described in "Pickwick Papers". Dickens says it was "very much like a perpendicular street a man sees in a dream, which he cannot get up for the life of him".

Royal Victoria Park (5): In 1619, Sir Nicholas Hyde, recorder of Bath, said that the Common Fields were for the use and enjoyment of the free burgesses inhabiting the city and should remain so forever.

In 1827, the Freemen, who were trustees of the land, applied to build houses and villas in the fields. The council refused, because of Sir Nicholas Hyde's decree that they should never be built on.

In 1829 a group of mainly businessmen proposed the formation of Ornamental Walks and Rides. The idea of the park was born.

The Park was opened in October 1830 by the 11-year old Princess Victoria who was on a visit to Bath.

There are many parks around the country named after Victoria, but this is the only Royal Victoria Park, because the Princess herself gave permission for the name.

The park was planted with over 25,000 trees and shrubs.

The obelisk was built in 1837 to commemorate the Princess's 18th birthday. It was dedicated on her coronation day, 28th June 1838.

Chapter One - Sidetracks

SIDETRACKS
Other places to discover in this part of town

The Gravel Walk behind Brock Street (6) - was laid out by John Wood the Younger as a sedan chair route.

Sion Hill (7) - opposite this house was once a greengrocers run by a man with the unusual name of Bedggood.

The Queen Square gate of Royal Victoria Park (8) is flanked by two lions. Legend says that the lions throw the balls across to each other as the clock strikes thirteen.

Chapter One - Sidetracks

Jupiter's Head (9) in The Great Dell of Royal Victoria Park (a former quarry) was added in 1839. It was carved by a self-taught mason, John Osborne, out of a single block of Bath Stone. The Shakespeare monument in this park was erected by Jerom Murch (1864) to celebrate the tercentenary of the playwrite's birth. This Unitarian minister and seven times mayor of Bath was a friend of William Beckford's and largely responsible for the layout and planting of this picturesque idyll. It is very probable therefore that Beckford himself contributed to the park's creation

Autumn & Spring in the Botanical Gardens (10 & 11), Royal Victoria Park. The summer pavilion (11) was Bath's exhibit at the British Empire Exhibition held at Wembley in 1924.

The Approach Golf Course on High Common (12) - is perfect for snow-boarding and sledding. The Freemen of Bath tried unsuccessfully to build a development in a style similar to Pittville in Cheltenham here in 1827.

Lansdown Crescent
Rural Retreat

Chapter Two

The North

Chapter Two - Introduction

Once John Wood the Younger had led the way with Royal Crescent, a perfect cascade of crescents sprung up along the contour lines of Bath's surrounding hills. On this northern slope, the most dramatic is the serpentine meandering of Lansdown Crescent. It is uncertain who was the architect, but he made a fine use of its commanding position. From here, at night, Bath looks like an open jewel-box, its contents spilling out, with the floodlit Abbey like a great diamond in the centre.

In 1823 Lansdown Crescent acquired a new resident who was certainly appreciative of stunning vistas. William Beckford, the eccentric owner of Fonthill Abbey, sold his Wiltshire estates and moved to No 20. He began to lease and buy property behind his house to lay out yet another estate here in Bath. It culminated in a tower where its owner could enjoy his works of art, read books and admire the view to all four points of the compass. The tower can still be viewed today, now restored to its Beckfordian splendour by Bath Preservation Trust.

As the Victorian age moved on, so did architectural style. Today the 19th century villas, which line the old turnpike road up Lansdown Hill, were mainly designed by the Bath architect James Wilson. He was also responsible for the fanciful St Stephen's church, and the main buildings of two major public schools, Bath Royal High School and Kingswood School.

With its views, sense of space and easy access to both city and motorway, this is still one of Bath's most fashionable areas.

WALK OVERVIEW:	See guide to The Walks on page three
Brock Street	St. Stephen's Church
Margaret's Buildings (25)	**Lansdown Crescent (10)**
Catherine Place	Lansdown Place West
Rivers Street	Park Street
Julian Road	**St. James's Square (24)**
Museum of Bath at Work (I)	Crescent Lane
Lansdown Road	Upper Church Street

Chapter Two

LANSDOWN CRESCENT

Lansdown Crescent began as a single house, which today is No. 1 Lansdown Crescent. The field in front used to be called Hilly Lydes.

In 1787 The developers Messrs Spackman and Lowder advertised for builders, describing the crescent they proposed as "so well suited that every part of the building will have the benefit of this pleasing distance of country which can never be intercepted by any building."

The residents of the crescent still enjoy the "most beautiful and extensive prospect of near twenty miles to the south and south west" mentioned in the advertisement.

The lamp-holders in front of each house are an original feature, mentioned in the deeds. They are now converted to electric light.

The architect is sometimes said to be John Palmer, but there is no evidence for this. It is possible that it was John Lowder himself, a banker and gentleman architect.

Chapter Two

There was a chapel for the residents, erected in 1794. It was called All Saints, and was built at the bottom of the field in front of the crescent so as to avoid blocking the view. It had a painted window by the well known Bath artist Thomas Barker, who lived at Doric House.

In 1799 there were complaints about the servants using the pews. It was badly damaged during World War II and demolished. Chapel House is all that remains. It is part of a house that went underneath the church and was intended for Charles Spackman. When he went bankrupt it was used instead by John Lowder.

Lansdown Crescent's most famous resident was William Beckford. Known as England's wealthiest son, he had previously lived in great affluence at Fonthill Bishop in Wiltshire. He purchased No. 20 Lansdown Crescent in 1823. He also owned No 1 Lansdown Place West and built the connecting bridge in the 1820s.

Chapter Two

BECKFORD'S TOWER

Beckford bought and leased land behind the houses all the way to the top of Lansdown. It included the present Dixon Gardens which was a fruit and vegetable garden.

On top of the hill he worked with the young architect Henry Edmund Goodridge to design a tower.

The Tower was originally not supposed to be as tall as it is today, but every time it reached the agreed height, Beckford insisted on going higher.

It is said that while Beckford was inspecting the building work on the tower, he noticed that he could no longer see Fonthills tower. It had collapsed, leaving just a heap of rubble.

Beckford came here every day, to read books, arrange flowers and admire his works of art. He also loved the wide-ranging views, which he said were "the finest in Europe."

From the top of the tower, on a clear day, the Bristol channel and Alfred's Tower at Stourhead can be seen.

Chapter Two

When Princess Victoria was visiting Bath in 1830 she was taken to see Beckford's Tower.

The tower had its own form of central heating. Heated air was directed up through the tower by a flue disguised as a beautiful vase, now missing but thought to be in Scotland.

The tower is now owned by Bath Preservation Trust and has recently been restored to its former glory with lottery money. This included gilding the top of the tower, as it was in Beckford's day. It is also now floodlit at night.

The Tower is open to the public and there is also a holiday apartment on the ground floor administered by the Landmark Trust.

The Tower Garden became Lansdown cemetery after Beckford's death and both he and Goodridge are buried here.

Chapter Two - The Walk

THE WALK
Places to discover on the Chapter Two Walk

Brock Street (1) was designed as a low-key connection between the two architectural masterpieces of The Circus and the Royal Crescent.

Rivers Street (3) is named after the family that ultimately owned much of this side of town.

Writer Fanny Burney (much admired by Jane Austen) and her emigré husband Count d'Arblay found Rivers Street too expensive and they had to move.

An analysis of the households on Rivers Street between 1851-81 showed that they employed an average of one resident female servant.

In Jane Austen's "Persuasion", Anne Elliot's friend Lady Russell lives on Rivers Street.

Chapter Two - The Walk

In the 1890's the Young Women's Friendly Society operated from premises on **Russel Street** (2). The YWFS aimed to provide "pleasant and domestic evenings for young women engaged in business or tuition."

Julian Road was formerly Cottle's Lane until the 19th century, when it was discovered it had been the Roman route from Sea Mills to Bath. The Victorians decided it was called the Via Julia – in fact the Romans just called it Highway 14.

Christ Church on Julian Road was built in 1798 – the first free church to be built in England since the Reformation. It was for the sake of the poor who could not pay pew rent.

The Museum of Bath at Work is housed in a tennis court built in 1777. It was for Real or Royal Tennis and was "respectably attended" when it opened. It was said to be based on the court owned by the Duke of Orleans in Paris.

Near the tennis court was a riding school where Jane Austen watched her friend Miss Chamberlayne "look hot on horseback".

St. Stephen's Church (5) was designed by James Wilson, St. Stephen's was initially completed in 1845. It was not consecrated until 1880 because the local bishop insisted it be oriented east-west.

Chapter Two - Sidetracks

Rivers Street (6) - The steps leading off the high pavement of Rivers Street were originally used to help mount horses. They also provided access down to the road. The Chequers on River Street is a local pub well worth visiting especially if you like a game of Pool.

Rear of Cavendish Place (7) - this Georgian terrace was designed by John Pinch in 1808.

Northampton Street (8) - the church at the end of Northampton Street was bombed heavily during the blitz and demolished.

Chapter Two - Sidetracks

Bath Racecourse at Lansdown (9). It was established in 1784 and the site is presently being redeveloped - racing starts at Easter and runs through to October with many different events throughout the season: A ladies day in June, family fun days in July and August and the Ladies Derby in the same month.

Antiquarian bookshop in Margaret's Buildings (10). Doric order column in Brock Street (11).

Alottment gardens off Richmond Lane (12) - looking towards the Millennium Garden on Richmond Road where there is a children's playground open to the public.

Chapter Three

The Northeast

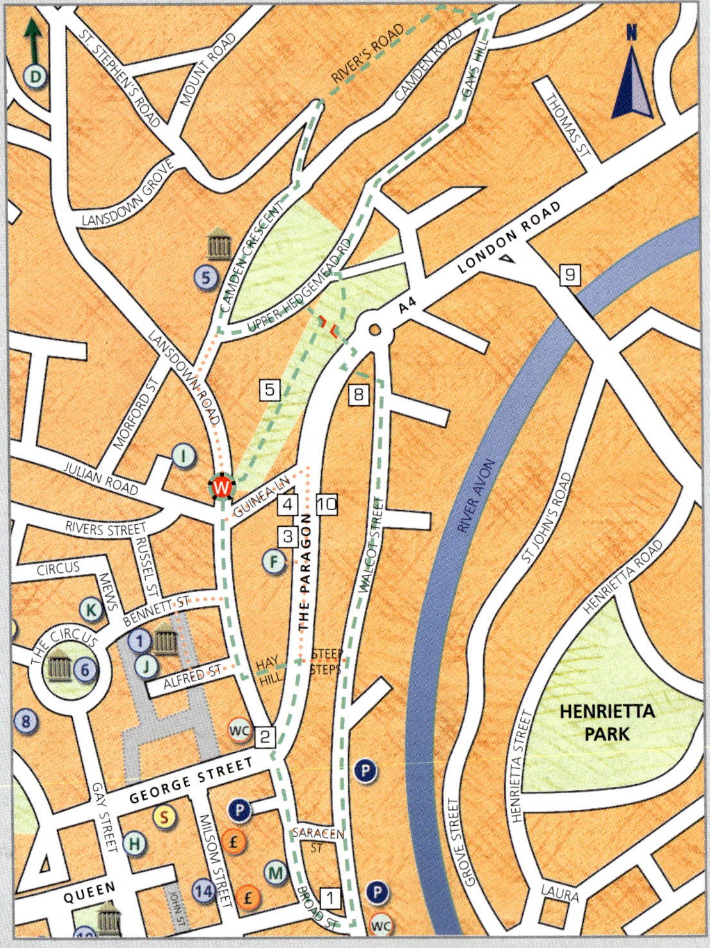

Chapter Three - Introduction

This north-east segment of the city is perhaps one of its most fascinating and varied quarters. Walcot Street itself was once the scene of a busy cattle market, one reminder being the ornate horse trough which also had a drinking fountain for human thirst. Most drovers, however, preferred the many pubs which lined the street. Sadly, only The Bell remains, but it is a focus for community events in the area. It is still a working area of town, with glass-making, pottery, tile-making and other crafts, but it was only during the 18th century that industry arrived. In the 17th century elegant houses stood here, their gardens going down to the river. Centuries before that, the Romans had a busy settlement outside the walls of their city of Aquae Sulis. At the far end of Walcot Street the parish church of St Swithin's stands, facing the steep slopes of Hedgemead Park, overlooked by Camden Crescent. While Camden Crescent was being built, a landslip stopped further development, leaving it looking lop-sided. However, later developers built on the hillside beneath it, until in the 1870s and 80s a series of disastrous slips resulted in most of the houses being demolished and the park being created in their place.

Walking along the Paragon, the visitor notices the Gothick fantasy of the Countess of Huntingdon's Chapel, now the home of Bath Preservation Trust and the Building of Bath Museum. A steep flight of steps links Paragon with Walcot or a fascinating selection of shops can be found in busy Broad Street leading back into the city.

With its associations with the Austen family, its ecclesiastical and industrial history, and its lively modern character, this is an area of great variety and vivacity.

WALK OVERVIEW:	
Hedgemead Park	Hedgemead Park
Upper Hedgemead Road	Walcot Street
Camden Crescent (5)	Broad Street
St. Stevens Road	**The Postal Museum (M)**
River's Road	The Paragon
Gay's Hill	**The Building of Bath Museum (F)**
Upper Hedgemead Road	Lansdown Road

Chapter Three

CAMDEN CRESCENT

Camden Crescent was designed by John Eveleigh and work started about 1788.

Its original name was Upper Camden Place and it was named after Charles Pratt, Marquis of Camden.

The Camden family crest is an elephant's head, and there is an elephant's head over each door. Clearly some of the stonemasons had never seen such an animal. Each one is different and they wear a variety of expressions from mischievous to downright disapproving.

After a large part of the crescent had been built there was a landslip and the eastern end had to be abandoned. This is why the "central" feature is not in the centre. For many years the last house was left standing as a picturesque Classical ruin.

Jane Austen features Camden Place as the lodgings for the Elliots in her book "Persuasion".

Chapter Three

Many architectural experts are offended by the five columns beneath the triangular pediment. Rules of taste dictate that there should be an even number. Certainly, seen from a distance, the crescent is oddly disturbing.

The first house, with the curved balcony, was the subject of a painting by Sickert and is called Sheepshank's House.

Above Camden Crescent and Road are the steep slopes of Beacon Hill. Here could be found Walcot Botanic Garden, where, in 1793, subscribers of half a guinea could walk the garden and inspect the plants. "For the gratification of the curious and public in general, a great variety of the newest and rarest Annual and Ornamental flowers and seeds will be raised ... at very moderate prices."

Chapter Three

WALCOT STREET

Walcot Street is one of the oldest streets in Bath. Although it was outside the city walls, it was heavily settled by the Romans and the local Celts.

Its name derives from wealh, the Saxon word for foreigner. This is also the word from which we get Wales and Cornwall.

In the 17th century the street was lined with large houses, their gardens leading down to the river.

By the end of the 18th century there was a mass of little courts and alleyways. They had names like "Hen and Chicken Court".

The southern end of Walcot Street was the market area, the charter having been granted by Edward III in 1317.

As recently as the early 1900s sheep pens filled the street on market days.

In 1855 a new market hall was opened to deter the farmers from doing business in pubs. To mark the occasion, the City Fathers went off to a celebratory lunch – at a Walcot Street pub, the Bladud's Head. Only the Bell now survives out of the many alehouses that lined this busy street.

Chapter Three

It was once said of the street that every other house was a pub. 21 pubs have been identified in this area, including the Hand & Shears, the Jolly Sailor, and the Don Cossack, as well as the better-known Three Cups, the Beehive and the Bell. The Pelican was the most famous and Dr. Johnstone drank there. Both the Bell and the Hat and Feather have regular live music.

Around 1900 another pub, the Catherine Wheel, offered its patrons "well-aired beds".

The horse trough was given to the city by Miss Elizabeth Landon. According to a guide of 1864 it is "composed of specimens from all the various building stones found in the immediate neighbourhood, with the addition of granite and white marble. The design is a most harmonious composition." The water is said to come from a spring called the Carn Well, which was famous for curing eye disorders.

Chapter Three - The Walk

THE WALK
Places to discover on the Chapter Three Walk

St Michael's Church (1) was built in 1835, but it was not the first church on the site. The first one was pulled down in 1734, and replaced by a Georgian one designed by a man called Harvey. John Wood said that it was so ugly that a horse, used to seeing good buildings, was so frightened by it that it had to be blindfolded to get it to go past. Its correct name is St Michael Without as it stood outside the city wall.

At the bottom of **Broad Street** (2) can be found the Saracen's Head. One of Bath's oldest pubs, Charles Dickens is reputed to have stayed here in 1835, when he came to Bath as a young reporter.

The **Building of Bath Museum** is housed in the former Countess of Huntingdon's Chapel (3) on The Paragon. Selina, Countess of Huntingdon, was a Methodist and friend of John Wesley's until they fell out over which one of them was to lead the movement. He said of her egotism: "She speaks of my college, my masters, my students: 'I' mixes with everything."

Chapter Three - The Walk

The Star public house (4) was erected and run by Daniel Aust, one of the builders of the Paragon. Here he paid his workmen, and saw the money he had paid out soon return to his pocket.

Daniel Aust also made coffins, which may explain the shape of the block that contains the pub.

The Star is one of the few pubs in the country to retain a Victorian interior and is on the CAMRA National Inventory of Historic Pub Interiors.

The hillside below Camden Crescent was once called Edgemead – but the mapmakers, thinking that the locals dropped their aitches, wrote it down as **Hedgemead** (5), the name it now bears.

During the 19th century narrow streets lined with houses were built on the steep slopes of Hedgemead. In the 1870s a series of landslips began, and in 1888 the council pulled down most of the buildings and opened Hedgemead Park (left) the next year. Only Gloster Villas and the flight of steps leading to now-vanished streets remain.

Chapter Three - Sidetracks

Richmond Road (6) is reputedly the longest uninterrupted stretch of Georgian houses in the country. The Richmond Arms is part of the terrace and has a good reputation for food. St Stephen's Primary School is opposite. At the southern end of the green a footpath leads down through the woods to Camden Road or Fairfield. From Richmond, a walk along Charlcombe Lane takes you to the pretty St Mary the Virgin church which has a holy well.

Larkhall (7) is one of Bath's villages. The original Lark Hall, a small Manor house, became a coaching inn, the Larkhall Inn, in 1784.

Chapter Three - Sidetracks

St. Swithin's Church (8), Walcot. Jane Austen's father George is buried in the crypt – the tombstone has been placed in the garden to one side where it can be seen today. The original building was a small village church and remnants of this can be found in the crypt. It was modernised by John Palmer in 1774 although the tower was built later in 1790. St Swithin was a loyal servant of the Kings of Wessex and became the patron saint of Winchester. Fanny Burney is buried in the Walcot Mortuary Chapel graveyard opposite

Cleveland Bridge (9). Designed by H.E. Goodridge, architect of Beckford's Tower, in 1827 in the Greek Revival style popular at that time. The Dispensary at Cleveland Place nearby provided medicines on a charitable basis.

The Paragon (10). To build The Paragon, the architect, Thomas Atwood, had to shore up the site with a huge wall. The Star pub on the north side has a listed interior and is an excellent real ale pub.

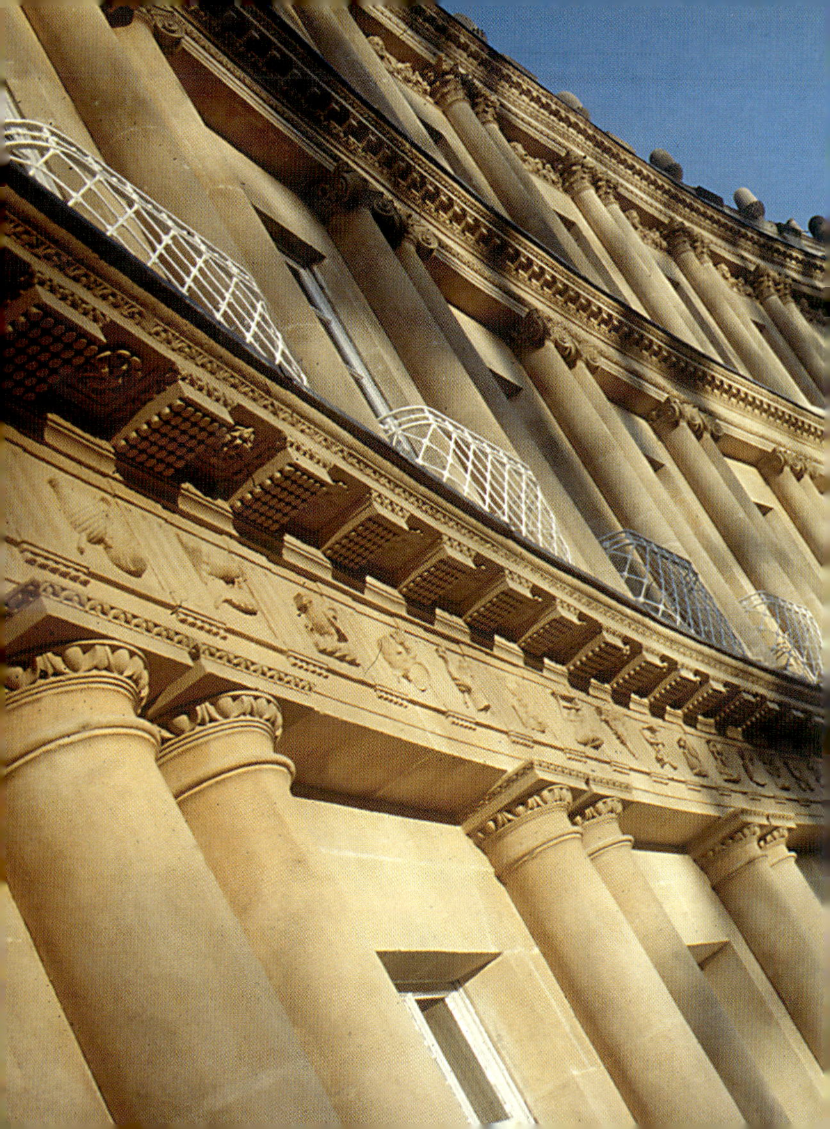

The Circus
A Vision of Rome

Chapter Four

North Central

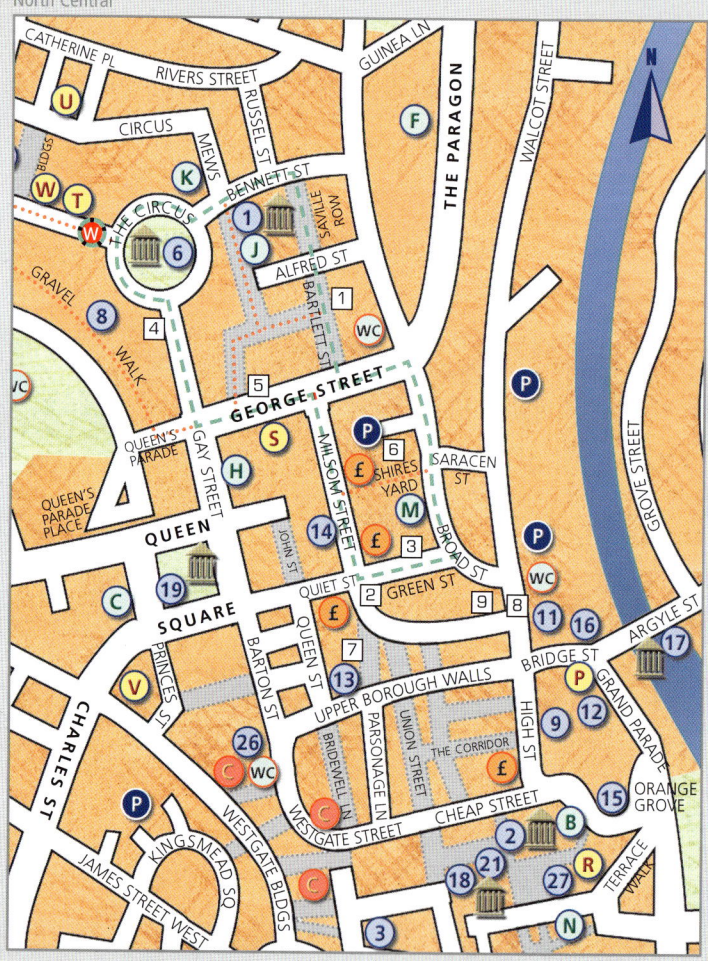

Chapter Four - Introduction

The Circus marks the apogee of John Wood the Elder's plans for Bath. Frustrated in his attempts to create a new Rome in this Somerset valley, he put many of his architectural and historical theories in this circle, sometimes described as the Coliseum turned inside out. Sadly, this creative if wayward and difficult man never saw his creation complete as he died at the age of 49. His son, also called John Wood, completed the work, and went on to build the Assembly Rooms on a rather cramped site to the east of the Circus. Now the home of the Museum of Costume, it was once the venue for glittering balls and masquerades. From the Assembly Rooms a footpath leads past the antiques markets into George Street. Opposite is the Royal York Hotel, newly restored and once again welcoming visitors from afar. The most illustrious in 1830 was the 11-year old Princess Victoria. During her stay in the city she opened the park and enjoyed an outing to Mr. Beckford's Tower. Later she was to recall the visit with great pleasure, in particular her ride in a sedan chair.

From the steps in front of Edgar Buildings, George Street, where the garrulous Isabella Thorpe was staying in "Northanger Abbey" there is a view down Milsom Street. Built as a street of houses in the 1760s, it had previously been a field where the weavers and dyers who worked in Broad Street dried their cloth on racks. Now it is one of Bath's principal shopping streets. It leads into the early 19th century New Bond Street which replaced the less elegantly named Frog Lane. To the north of New Bond Street and easily missed is Green Street, with its muddle of early 18th century houses designed by local builders who ignored the principles of classical architecture.

WALK OVERVIEW:

The Circus (6)	Broad Street
Bennett Street	**The Postal Museum (M)**
Assembly Rooms (1)	Green Street
Museum of Costume (J)	**Milsom Street (14)**
Saville Row	George Street inc. Edgar Bdgs.
Bartlett Street	Gay Street
George Street	

Chapter Four

THE CIRCUS

The Kings Circus was begun in 1754 but not finished until 1766, work ceasing for several years due to an economic recession.

The architect was John Wood the Elder, but he died in 1754 and the work was carried out by his son.

As part of his schemes for a new Rome in the Avon Valley, Wood conceived the idea of a circular building as an Imperial Gymnasium, where games could be held in the centre. However, the City Council dismissed these plans as "chimerical". Instead he designed this circular terrace of 33 houses.

There are three evenly spaced entrances into the Circus. Draw an imaginary line to join them and you have the Masonic symbol of a triangle in a circle, representing the Trinity in Eternity.

Although the segments are equal the houses are not. There are 11 in the western section, 10 to the north and 12 in the south eastern one.

John Wood was fascinated by stone circles such as Stonehenge in Wiltshire. The Circus is his own version of

Chapter Four

a stone circle, and has the same diameter as the encircling grass rampart at Stonehenge.

On the face of the building can be seen the three classic orders of architecture. At the lowest level are Doric columns, above them, with the scrolls, are Ionic columns, and at the top level are Corinthian columns, crowned with acanthus leaves.

Encircling the Circus above the Doric columns are over 500 carvings. Some indicate the occupation of the first resident of the house, others are Masonic, but many come from a 17th century children's book. Among them are a crocodile, a dolphin and the four winds.

Among the famous people who stayed in the Circus were Thomas Gainsborough, William Pitt the Elder, David Livingstone and Clive of India. Not all were impressed with it. Elizabeth Montagu, Queen of the Blue Stockings, called it a nest of boxes.

In Circus Mews there were two pubs for the thirsty servants of the inhabitants of the Circus.

Chapter Four

MILSOM STREET

Named after the leaseholder of the land Daniel Milsom, this was built in the early 1760s as a street of houses. Very quickly the shops and banks spotted a good site and began to move in.

The field on which it was built was the rack field. Here stood the racks or drying frames for the cloth woven in Broad Street. Another name for a rack was a tenter. Cloth was stretched tightly on these hooks, hence the term "on tenterhooks".

In 1781 Thomas Baldwin, the city architect, built Somersetshire Buildings on the site of the old poor-house in the middle of the east side of Milsom Street.

Chapter Four

ASSEMBLY ROOMS

Designed by John Wood the Younger, work commenced on these rooms in 1769 and they opened in 1771.

This is Bath's only surviving set of Assembly Rooms. The most fashionable rooms burnt down in 1820, and the other set near Parade Gardens were demolished in the early 19th century.

Originally called the New or Upper Rooms, they were financed by a tontine. A tontine is a system where, as shareholders die, their shares go into the pot until the surviving shareholder takes everything. Among the shareholders were Lord Clive, Mr Leigh Perrot, and William Hoare, the Bath artist.

Bath's most famous Master of Ceremonies, Beau Nash, was dead by the time these Upper Assembly Rooms were built. His successor was Captain Wade whose portrait by Thomas Gainsborough can still be seen at these Assembly Rooms today.

Balls were on Mondays and Thursdays and among the musicians were William Herschel and his brother Alexander, James Cantelo, who came from a family that still lives in Bath, and Elizabeth Linley, who married Richard Sheridan.

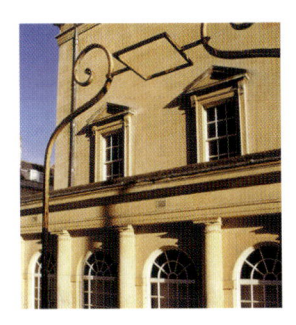

Chapter Four - The Walk

THE WALK
Places to discover on The Chapter Four Walk

Established in 1984 and containing 25 dealers and 55 cabinets, the **Bartlett Street** Antiques Centre is one of the largest of its kind and the largest in Bath.

Green Street (2) is named after the bowling green that stood outside the city walls before the 18th century. The pub, The Old Green Tree, is said to commemorate the tree that shaded the green.

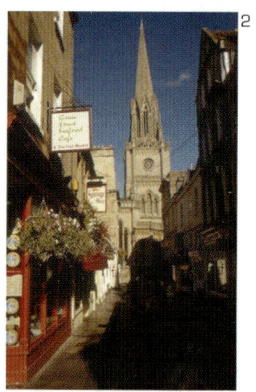

On the corner of the street once stood The Oliver (now St Christopher's Inn) named after Doctor William Oliver who invented the dry biscuit that bears his name. Invented as a cure for his gouty patients, it helped to make his fortune and he died a wealthy man.

Many of the buildings were erected by men who had read about Palladian architecture but did not understand the principals. This explains the uneven appearance of the façades.

On the north side is a house dating from 1716, looking much like a Cotswold farmhouse but with a fine shell-canopy over the door. The Old Green Tree (3) is a small but excellent pub that serves lunch.

Chapter Four - The Walk

Gay Street (4) was originally called Barton St (also spelled Berton) but was renamed after the London Surgeon, Robert Gay, who owned the land on which it was built.

The intriguing building at the north-east corner of Queen Square, No 41 Gay Street was built for Richard Merchant. The house has an interesting design with diagonally positioned main rooms, one of which was designed as a place to powder your wig. In 1797 annual rent in Gay St. was approximately £160. Today a ground floor would cost £14000 p.a.

No. 11 **George Street** (5) has an Art Nouveau shop window (1907) with bevelled plate glass decorative lights which are almost irreplaceable.

Chapter Four - Sidetracks

Shires Yard (6) was originally stables built by Walter Wiltshire in the 1740s for his carting & carrying business. Wiltshire lent Thomas Gainsborough a horse for the painting "The Harvest Wagon" which Gainsborough then gave to Wiltshire. The yard linking Milsom Street to Broad Street is now a shopping development specialising in fashion and luxury goods. A French Café and The Moon and Sixpence restaurant allow customers to eat al fresco in the courtyard and both The Postal Museum and the Podium with car parking are easily accessible from here.

Old Bond St (7). It was here that in Jane Austen's "Persuasion" Sir Walter Elliot stood in a shop and counted 87 women go by "without there being a tolerable face among them". Certainly not the case today. At the end is The Royal Mineral Water Hospital (1735).

Chapter Four - Sidetracks

Inside The Podium on Northgate St. (8). This very short street marks the site of the Northgate. It was taken down in 1755 as part of a road-widening scheme. The Podium houses the supermarket Waitrose and many specialist shops. The public library and a wide rage of restaurants are all on the second floor of this post modern building.

Post Office window, New Bond St. (9) The building stands on the site of a large coaching inn called The Castle and Ball. Ralph Allen, the builder of Prior Park made his fortune by revolutionising the postal service. The first postage stamp in the world was sent from Bath on the 2nd May 1840. Visit the Postal Museum at No. 8 Broad Street for further information. If you miss the last post here you can take mail to the sorting office near Bath Spa station. Bath has many historic post boxes from different periods. See Quiz at back of book.

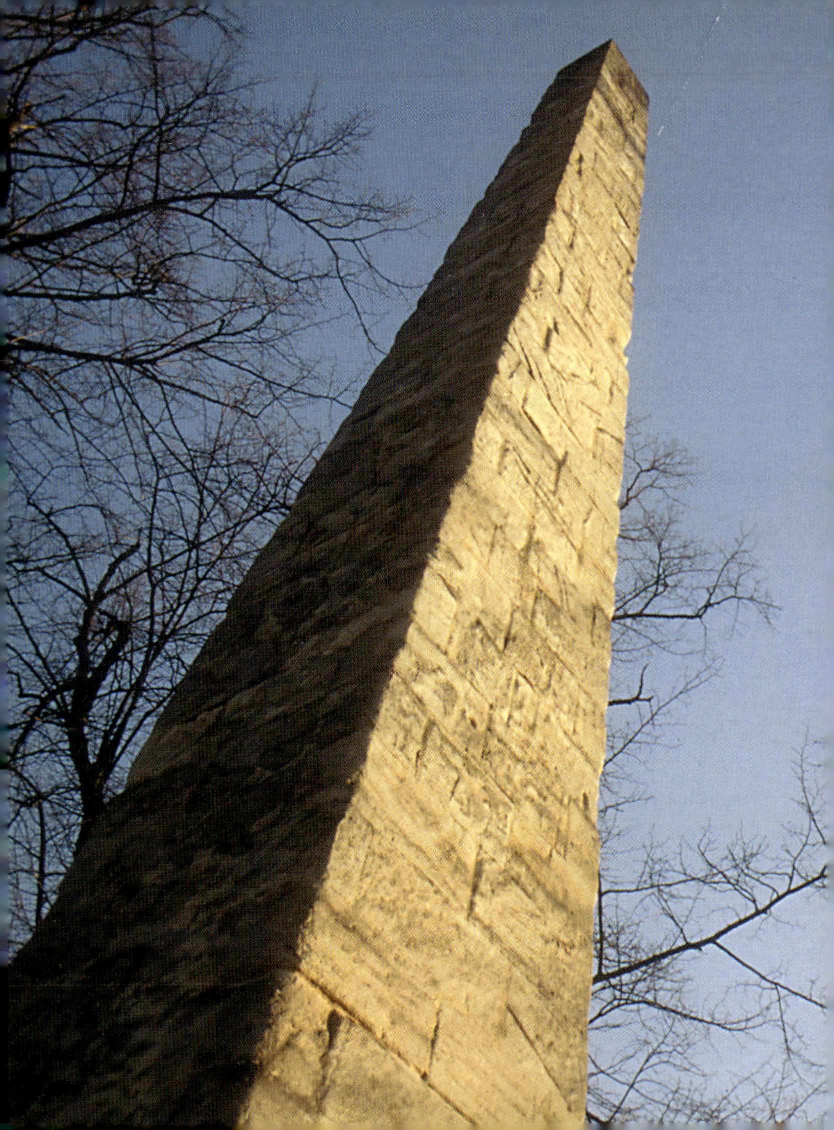

Queen Square
Reaching for the Sky

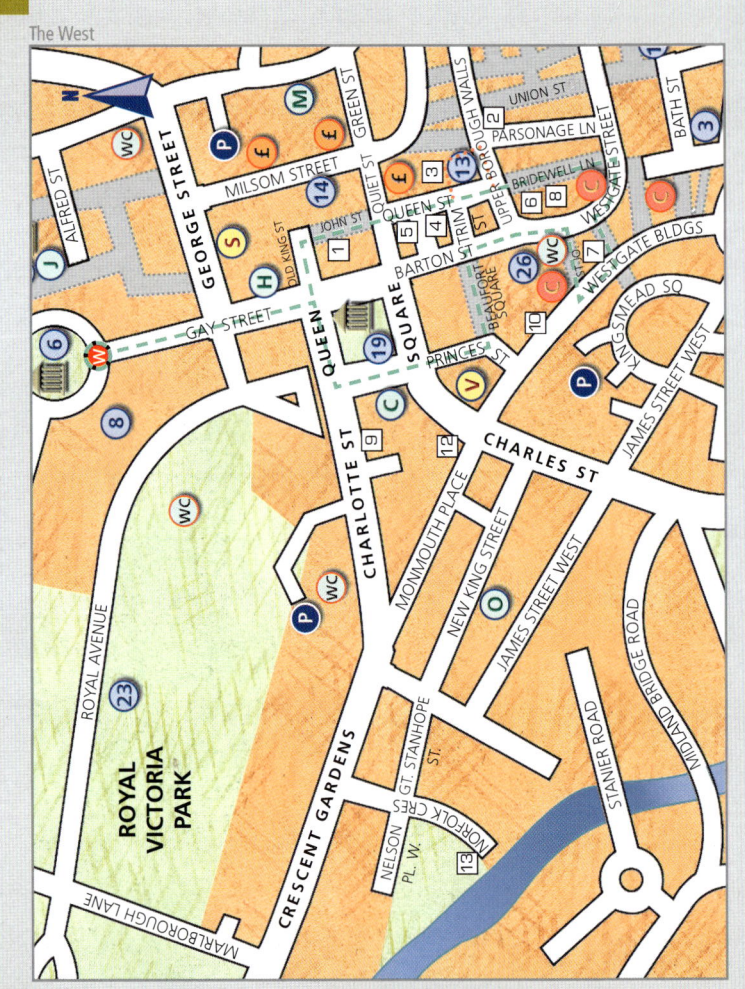

Chapter Five

The West

Chapter Five - Introduction

The visitor who turns out of Milsom Street along the curiously named Quiet Street will soon arrive in the imposing surroundings of Queen Square. Named after Queen Caroline, the wife of George II, it was intended to resemble a palace and its courtyard. Victorian tree-planting and modern traffic have deprived the square of its impact, but in 1734, when it was just completed, it was revolutionary. For the first time in Bath, Palladian architecture had made its appearance in the city. As the architect John Wood himself said, "it may be looked upon as a perfect sample of a well-regulated place." Sadly, a hundred years later it was regarded as rather antiquated, and the west side was dramatically altered when a building in the very latest style, the Greek revival, was forced in between two John Wood villas.

By contrast, Trim Street, which is earlier, is another example of the attempts of local builders to build in the latest fashion without really understanding how it worked. Best among them is No. 5, known as General Wolfe's House, with its martial trophies over the door added after the battle of Quebec.

Not far from Trim Street is the Theatre Royal. Here world-famous actors tread the same stage as celebrated thespians of the past such as Sarah Siddons and Henry Irving.

To the west of Queen Square, those with connections but not sufficiently deep pockets could live in genteel but very much smaller premises, in streets such as New King Street and Great Stanhope Street. Here William Herschel lived with his sister Caroline as a struggling musician, before his skill as an astronomer reached the ears of King George III.

WALK OVERVIEW:	
Gay Street	St. John's Place
Jane Austen Museum (H)	Monmouth Street
Queen Square (19)	Westgate Street
Princes Street	Bridewell Lane
Beaufort Square	Trim Bridge & Queen Street
Barton Street & Saw Close	John Street
Theatre Royal (26)	Old King Street

Chapter Five

QUEEN SQUARE

Queen Square is the first major work by John Wood the Elder, built between 1728 and 1735. It is named after Queen Caroline, wife of George II.

It was built in the style of Palladio who followed the principles of Vitruvius.

It is not as Wood first intended; it was too expensive to level the site, and the west side was not a terrace. Instead there were what appeared to be three great houses: two at each end and one set back in the middle. The two end ones survive, but in 1830, when these houses were just considered rather old-fashioned, the central one was removed and the Greek Revival block designed by Pinch the Younger replaced it.

Although the north side has the "elegance and grandeur of a palace", it is actually seven houses, many of which were lodging houses.

Chapter Five

John Wood lived at No. 9 (although a plaque on the north side states otherwise), in the centre of the south side so he could look out of his window and admire his Palladian palace.

In 1731, Wood was persuaded to help a woman he calls Sylvia. She had fallen on hard times due to her compulsive gambling, but Wood treated her as a trusted friend. Some say there was even a romantic attachment between them. However, while Wood and his wife were away in London, she dressed herself all in white and hanged herself with a silken girdle. Her ghost is said to walk the house.

The obelisk commemorates the visit to Bath of Frederick, Prince of Wales, in 1738. Richard "Beau" Nash nagged the poet Alexander Pope to provide an inscription for the obelisk. Thinking it beneath his dignity but wary of offending the King of Bath, Pope finally came up with the rather less than poetical: In memory of honours conferred and in gratitude for benefits bestowed in this city by his Royal Highness Frederick, Prince of Wales, and his Royal Consort, in MDCCXXXVIII this obelisk is erected by Richard Nash Esq.

Wood was very proud of the obelisk, which originally went to a point and stood 21.3m (70ft) high. A boules championship takes place here in the summer.

Jane Austen stayed at No. 13 when visiting Bath with her brother Edward. She said they were exceedingly pleased with the house.

Chapter Five

THEATRE ROYAL

Bath's Theatre Royal was the first outside London. It was a small building in Orchard Street, and by 1805 it was decided to move to Beaufort Square.

What is now the north side was the original entrance, designed by George Dance. The masks in the entablature above the windows are Comedy, Tragedy, and Satire. Lyres represent music, and the façade is crowned appropriately with the Royal Coat of Arms.

In 1823 a farce whose cast included two prizefighters proved very popular. It was called The Adventures of Tom and Jerry.

Beaufort Square was built around 1737 by the Bristol architect John Strahan. John Wood hated Strahan and described Beaufort Square as "piratical".

Chapter Five - The Walk

THE WALK
Places to discover on the Chapter Five Walk

Quiet Street commemorates the wife of one of John Wood's workmen who was an unusually silent woman.

Quiet Street is watched over by three statues on a building originally called The Bazaar, and dating from 1824. Two are Commerce and Genius, while no one seems to be certain what the third represents.

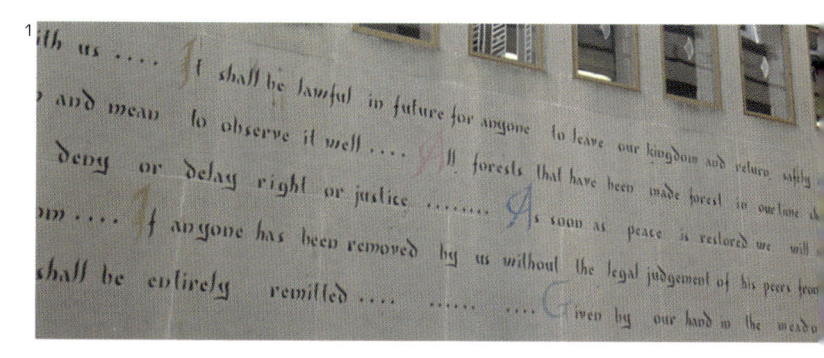

...ith us .... It shall be lawful in future for anyone to leave our kingdom and return safely ... and mean to observe it well .... All forests that have been made forest in our time sh... deny or delay right or justice .... As soon as peace is restored we will ... . If anyone has been removed by us without the legal judgement of his peers from ... shall be entirely remitted .... Given by our hand in the meado...

On the wall of a modern building in **John Street** (1) can be found extracts from the Magna Carta. The Bath connection is that one of the signatories was Jocelyn, Bishop of Bath and Glastonbury.

Among the new rules that the charter introduced was that no widow could be forced to marry against her wishes.

The Royal National Hospital for Rheumatic Diseases, in **Upper Borough Walls** (2 & 3), was founded in 1735 for poor people from outside of Bath. The doctor in charge was Doctor Oliver, better known as the inventor of the Bath Oliver biscuit.

Chapter Five - The Walk

The R.N.H.R.D. (2) was originally called the General Hospital, it is known locally as the Mineral Water hospital or even "the Min."

The parable of the Good Samaritan is depicted on the Victorian extension to the hospital.

A small portion of the old city wall (3) survives in Upper Borough Walls.

On the north side of the wall stood a small burial ground for the hospital. There were 17 mass graves, and by the time the ground was closed in 1849 (from regard for the health of the living, says the memorial plaque) 10 were full, one had three interments, and one contained the body of Phoebe Hayes. She had contracted smallpox, and was isolated from the other patients even in death.

John Wood tells us that **Trim Street** (4) was begun in 1707 and contains 18 houses. The land belonged to Mr Trim and "from him the street had its name."

Trim Street was built outside the city wall and a bridge was necessary to

Chapter Five - The Walk

cross over the lane in the dip behind the wall. It is commemorated today in the street that leads from Upper Borough Walls to Trim Street, called Trim Bridge.

The arch that passes across Queen Street as it enters Trim Street is sometimes mistakenly thought to be Trim Bridge. In fact its name is St John's Gate.

In 1757 Mr and Mrs Wolfe's son came to stay while he took the waters. He was, of course, General Wolfe. Shortly afterwards he went to Canada and defeated the French at Quebec. The carving over the doorway (5) reminds us of his triumph.

Trim Street was the last home in Bath of Mrs Austen and her daughters Jane and Cassandra, before leaving for Jane's beloved Hampshire.

Sawclose (6) was once called Timber Green, and was a busy workplace, including being a timber yard. It was also where sporting gentlemen of the 17th century could find the cockpit. The building which probably housed it survives as the bar Delfter Krug.

A tower, called Gascoyne's Tower, stood at the corner of Sawclose, on the old city wall. It was finally removed in the 1770s.

Chapter Five - Sidetracks

The Seven Dials complex, adjacent to the Theatre Royal, includes a fountain around which famous actors and actresses - including Nigel Hawthorne, Edward Fox, Susan Hampshire, Penelope Keith, Hayley Mills and Maureen Lipman - have made hand-prints (7).

The tower of the Bluecoat School, Sawclose (8), looking south with Macaulay Buildings in the background. The Jacobethan style was very popular in the 19th century when this was designed by Manners.

The former Moravian Church (9) near Queen Square was designed by James Wilson in 1845. The Moravians built a number of "utopian settlements" throughout Britain, including Fulneck in Yorkshire. It is very Roman in its boldness and composition. Tea is available at certain times. The architect also built St Stephen's church, Lansdown which is in the gothic style. Charlotte Street leads to Upper Bristol Road and this is one way to visit Norfolk Crescent and Victoria Park amusement facilities. The car parking opposite the church is ideal for the city centre or visiting the Royal Crescent.

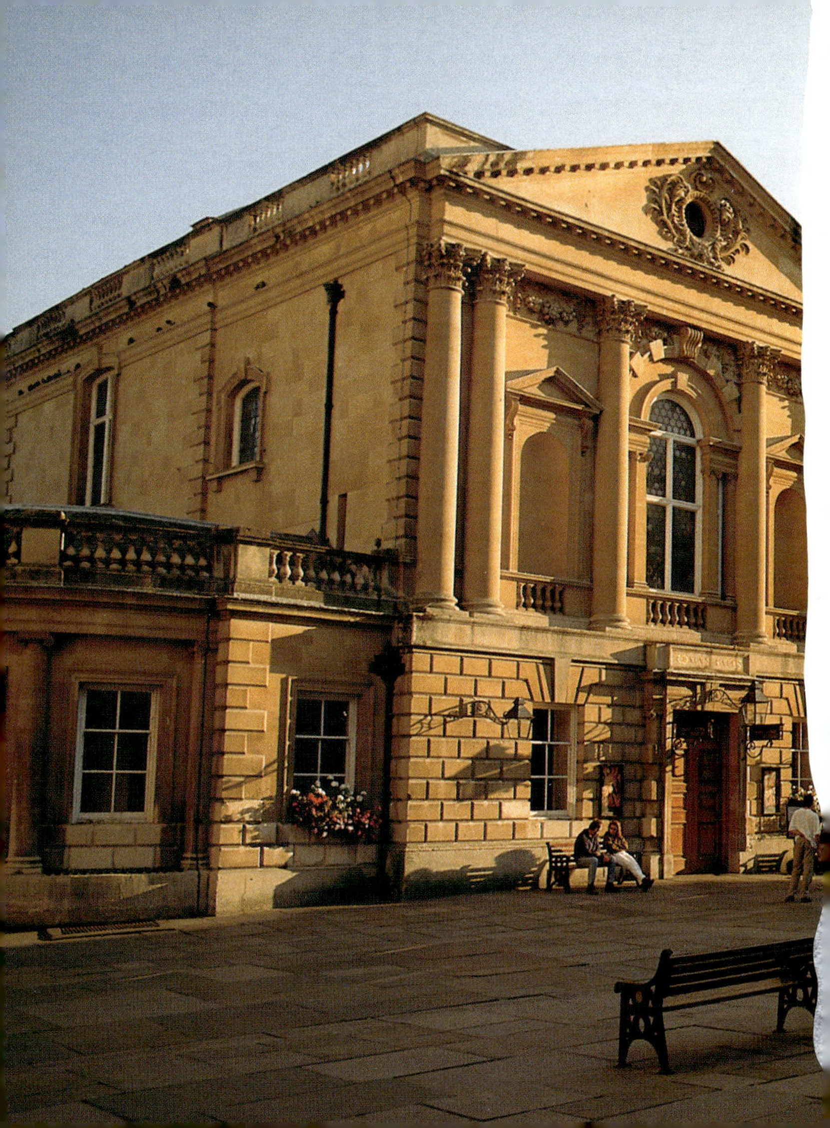

Chapter Five - Sidetracks

The Ustinov Studio (10). These old scenery storage rooms (formerly stables) were converted into a 140 seat theatre with the aid of lottery money. Sir Peter Ustinov helped raise the money and opened this new annex to the Theatre Royal in January 1998.

George III gave the Theatre (11) its Royal patent. The original entrance was in Beaufort Square. Beau Nash Lived in the house next door from 1720.

Bombed in the Baedeker raids of 1942, St Pauls was restored and renamed Holy Trinity Church (12) in 1952. 417 people were killed in Bath during the air raids.

Norfolk Crescent (13) was started in 1792 but by 1810 only nine of the proposed 19 buildings were finished.

The Roman Baths
Classic Triumph

Chapter Six

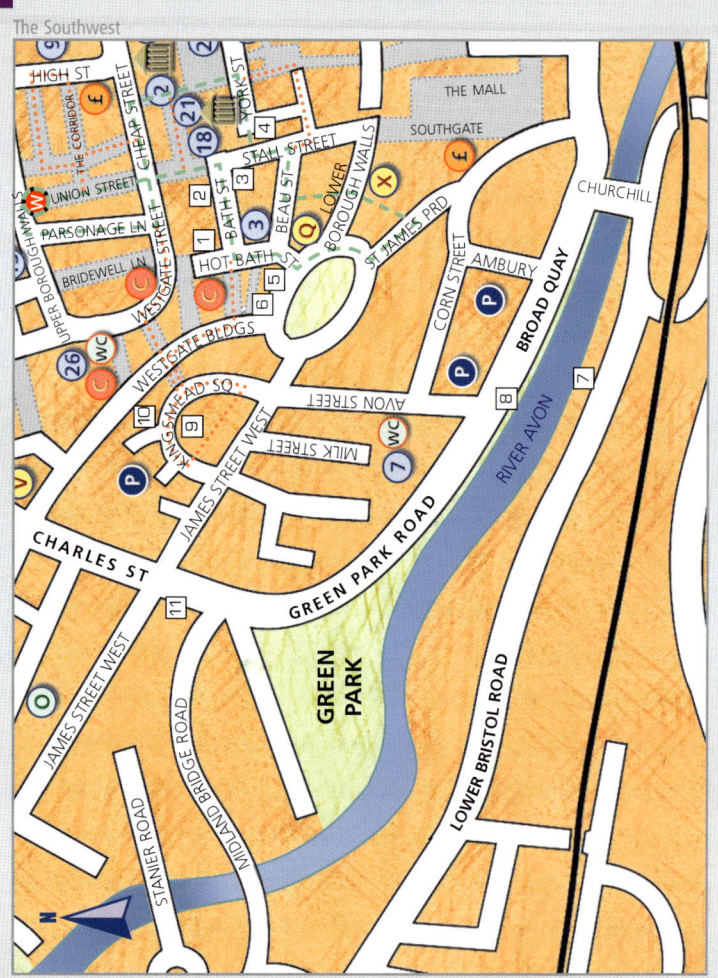

The Southwest

Chapter Six - Introduction

This area is the heart of the city and contains the reason for the its existence – the hot springs. From the time when an unknown Celt discovered that the water bubbling at his feet was hot to the modern tourists who wander through the city's streets, visitors have come here to take the waters – and enjoy themselves. Where elegant Bath Street now stands, Iron Age man came down from his hillfort home to call upon Sulis, the goddess of the springs. Beneath Stall Street lie the extensive suites of baths adjoining the temple dedicated to Sulis Minerva where Romans could worship, be shaved and enjoy a sauna all under the one roof. In the 17th century Anne of Denmark, wife of James I, came to the King's Bath, only to be frightened by a flame which rose from the spring. Here the 18th century visitors flirted with "darting, killing glances" while being serenaded by musicians. In the Pump Room, it was the custom to drink three glasses of water. And here too a new spa, Thermae Bath Spa, has risen from the remains of the old.

Rich and poor have always rubbed shoulders in Bath, and streets which were originally built to attract visitors became poor parts of Bath – Avon Street and Corn Street for example. In houses liable to be flooded when the river rose lived those who provided the labour for the great service industry that drove Bath. Yet just a stone's throw away was Green Park Buildings, where Jane Austen's family lived for a time. Jane was rightly suspicious of "the Damps" in this area, but the flood prevention scheme of the 1970s has removed the worst dangers. It involved the removal of Bath's Old Bridge, with its five arches.

WALK OVERVIEW: *See guide to The Walks on page three*

Union Street	Stall Street
Bath Street	York Street
Hot Bath Street	Abbey Church Yard
Thermae Bath Spa (3)	**Bath Abbey (2)**
St. James Parade	**Roman Baths (21) & Pump Room (18)**
Across Lower Borough Walls	Cheap Street & Westgate Street
Beau Street	Parsonage Lane

Chapter Six - The Roman Baths

ROMAN BATHS

The Romans built the first city here, around the sacred spring. They called it Aquae Sulis, the waters of Sulis, after the Celtic goddess of the spring.

Over the centuries the Roman Baths were forgotten until 1754, when the Duke of Kingston's workmen, digging out a new suite of baths, uncovered them. It was not until the 19th century that the extent of the baths was revealed.

Even today, Bath Archaeological Trust discovers more and more of the Roman city.

The Great Bath, the focal point of the Roman Baths, is about 25 metres long and 11 metres wide. It is lined with lead, which was mined on the Mendip Hills by Roman slaves.

The Roman Baths site covers an area amounting to 2 football pitches.

Roman citizens did not just bathe in the waters. Here, to the temple of Sul Minerva, they brought votive offerings of coins and carved jewels- and also curses, scratched on lead.

Sulis Minerva was a goddess created out of the Celtic and the Roman goddesses of healing. The

Chapter Six - The Roman Baths

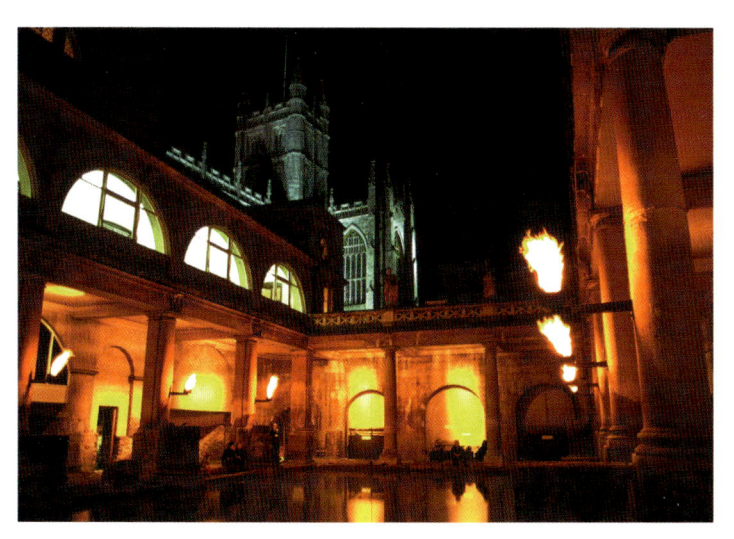

head of her statue was discovered beneath Stall Street in 1727. The rest has never been found.

The centrepiece of the temple pediment was a magnificently fierce face, the head entwined with snakes once described as the Gorgon's Head, made by an untutored Celtic craftsman, it is now thought it may be a sun god.

There are three main springs in the city, each of which has been used for bathing since Roman times.

Chapter Six - The Roman Baths

In the 16th century the baths were cleaned once a week, but by the late 17th century the baths were emptied every day. The scum, which still gathers on the water if it is left, was removed, as it was regarded as being too strong in chemicals to touch the skin.

When drinking the waters became part of the daily round, the first Pump Room was built, in 1706. It was replaced in 1795 by the present room.

Three glasses of mineral water a day at three different times was considered to be the usual amount one should take.

The pumper rented the right to sell the waters from the council. Today there is once again an official pumper. He is employed by the company that operates the restaurant, under contract to the council.

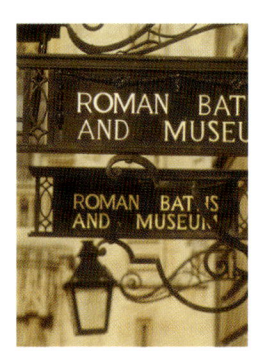

Thomas Tompion, the famous watchmaker, gave a clock and a sundial to the Pump Room, both of which can still be seen today.

Also in the Pump Room is the statue of Richard "Beau" Nash with plans for the General hospital He is Bath's most famous Master of Ceremonies.

Richard Nash brought to Bath the band of musicians to play in the Pump Room. Now reduced to a trio, musicians can still be heard in the Pump Room daily.

Chapter Six - The Roman Baths

The King's Bath was the most popular. It had a structure in the middle known as the Kitchen, where cripples who were cured used to hang their discarded crutches.

The bath is presided over by a statue of King Bladud, legendary founder of the city.

Adjoining the King's Bath was a smaller bath known as the New or Women's Bath. In 1615 Queen Anne of Denmark, wife of James I of England was about to step into the King's Bath when a flame leapt up from the spring and travelled across the water. The queen retreated to the smaller bath which henceforth was known as The Queen's Bath. It was taken down in the late 19th century to reveal the Roman Bath beneath.

Chapter Six - The Roman Baths

The King's Bath was built over the reservoir constructed by the Romans to contain the sacred spring. Its water level has now been lowered to where it was originally.

Bathers entered the baths by steps known as slips, while onlookers watched and gossiped from galleries above.

Celia Fiennes, who visited in 1687, tells us that the ladies wore garments made of a fine yellow canvas with large sleeves. The gentlemen, she says, wore drawers and waistcoats of the same yellow fabric. The iron in the waters would turn any other coloured clothes yellow anyway.

She also says that the water tastes like that in which you have boiled eggs. 150 years later, Dickens had Sam Weller describe it as having a strong flavour of warm flat irons.

During the 17th and 18th centuries The Cross Bath (right) was perhaps the most fashionable. Here Samuel Pepys saw some very fine ladies, although he did say "Methinks that it cannot be clean to go so many bodies together in to the same water."

Ned Ward, writing in 1700, went to the Cross Bath and saw "Wanton Dalliancies. Celebrated Beauties, Panting Breasts, and Curious Shapes almost exposed to public view; Languishing Eyes, darting Killing Glances.. attended by soft Musick."

The bath (right) is named after the cross that stood in the centre of the bath. One legend says it was set up in 709 when the body of St Adhelm was rested here on its way to back to Malmesbury for burial.

Chapter Six - The Roman Baths

The old cross was replaced in the late 17th century after Mary of Modena, wife of James II had successfully given birth to an heir. She had relied on the Cross Bath's fame as a cure for infertility.

The new cross, set up by the Earl of Melfort, gave great offence to Protestant citizens. Their expressions of disapproval, which consisted of battering bits of the cross, made the council carry out some "repairs" in 1744. Mysteriously, the most offending parts were "misplaced" by the workmen, so that it became more acceptable to Puritan sensibilities. It was finally taken down in 1784 when Thomas Baldwin completely remodelled the bath. One of the cherubs still exists in a niche over a shop in Milsom Street (Mallory's).

The spring for The Hot Bath rises beneath the street that runs in front of the present bath. It was here that the original building stood.

Before John Wood the Younger remodelled the bath in 1776 and moved the front to its present location, there were two baths here, the Hot Bath and the Lepers' Bath.

John Leland, writing in 1540, said the water in the Hot Bath would scald the flesh at first, "but after that the flesh is warmed it is more tolerable and pleasant."

The new Thermae Bath Spa complex features three baths: the renovated Hot Bath (mentioned above); the also renovated and open-air Cross Bath, which is a Grade 1 Listed building; and the brand new New Royal Bath, which was designed as a "glass cube" (above) by the Architectural firm Nicholas Grimshaw & Partners..

Chapter Six - The Walk

THE WALK
Places to discover on the Chapter Six Walk

Bath Street (1, 2 & 3): This graceful colonnaded street was built in the 1790s to replace the narrow lanes, which led between the King's Bath and the other two baths.

It was designed by Thomas Baldwin, one of the last pieces of work he carried out for the council before his money troubles lost him the post of City Architect.

The last house in Bath Street, next to the Hot Bath, was built in 1800 as the city museum. On its front there are two statues. Said variously to be from the Northgate, the Southgate or the old Market Hall, they appear to be a knight and a king or churchman. One statue still bears the remnants of the paint with which they were originally decorated.

St John's Hospital (5 & 6) was built in the 12th century as a refuge for 12 poor people of the city.

In the early 1720s the Duke of Chandos, displeased with his lodgings in what is now the hospital, saw an opportunity to make money in the newly fashionable city by providing better lodgings. He took leases on the properties, and employed John Wood to remodel the buildings, also rebuilding the rooms for the poor inhabitants.

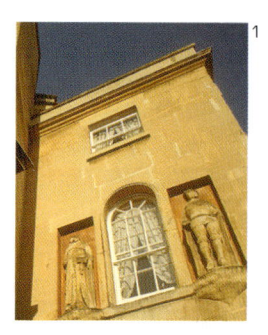

Chapter Six - The Walk

While the buildings were an improvement, the Duke had insisted on the installation of that new invention, the water closet. Unfortunately Wood was not very experienced with these, and a continual complaint from tenants, almsfolk and the Duke was about the smelly drains.

The classical bridge above York Street (4) was built by Major Davis to hide pipes for a laundry.

Abbey Church House: This building is one of the few Tudor houses left after the great rebuilding in the 18th century. It was built over a medieval building that was part of St John's Hospital. Erected around 1590 by Dr Baker, the house eventually came to Mrs Saville in 1691 who ran it as a successful lodging house.

The clock tower (6) and chapel of St Michael in St John's courtyard (5) was built in 1716 to a design by Killigrew.

Chapter Six - Sidetracks

The River Avon was made navigable in 1727 from Bristol to Bath. This link to a major port which itself had strong links to the rest of the world transformed the City. The very idea itself was a catalyst to John Wood the Elder who began his inspirational plans for Bath shortly after news broke that the scheme was to go ahead in 1725. Bath stone and beer (for the South Wales coalfields) in particular were shipped to Bristol.

River Walk (8). This part of the river had many factories and mills beside it. Some of the buildings still survive today (7).

Chapter Six - Sidetracks

Kingsmead Square (9 & 10). Named after the King's Meadows on which it stood, this square was largely designed by John Strahan. It caused John Wood considerable amusement because the builders ignored attempts at symmetry. He said the houses "have nothing, save ornaments without taste, to please the eye." Rosewell House (9) is in the flamboyant Baroque style which is unusual in Bath. The area has been revitalised by the nearby multiplex cinema and restaurants and cafes thrive here. The Jazz Cafe (10) serves a brilliant all day English breakfast.

Green Park Station (11 & 12). The most famous service to run through here was Somerset & Dorset's Pines Express that ran from Bournemouth to Bath, before going on to Liverpool and Manchester.

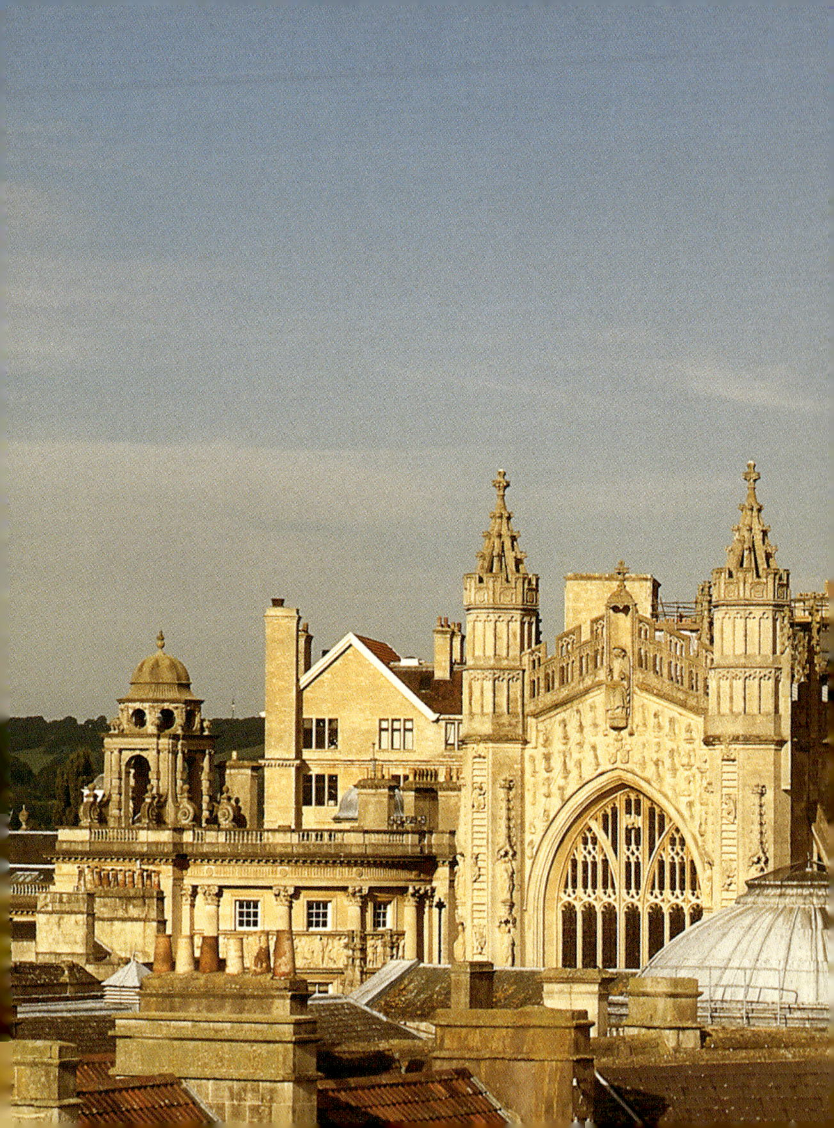

Bath Abbey
Gothic Glory

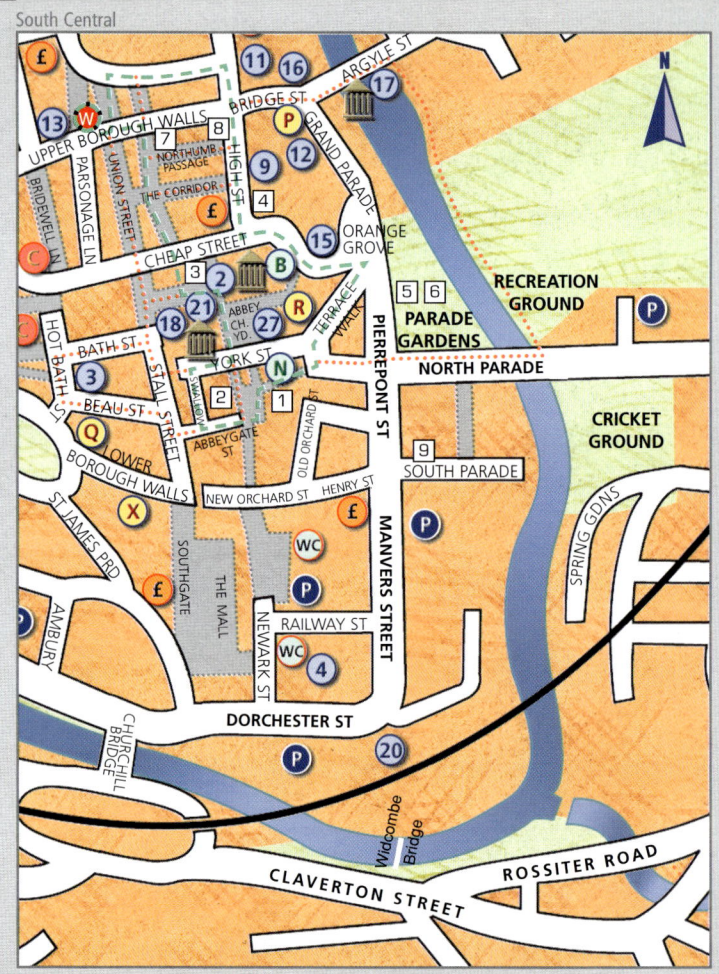

Chapter Seven

South Central

Chapter Seven - Introduction

The story of the Abbey is inextricably bound with that of the springs. It was the healing properties of the waters that led John of Tours, the Norman bishop, to build his cathedral here. The earlier Saxon Abbey was built on the site of a Roman temple. The present Abbey, commenced in 1499, is full of memorials to those who proved that Bath's waters were not an infallible cure. In the 18th century the area around the Abbey was the very centre of Georgian life. Here in the early morning they would come to the Pump Room for the first glass of water before seeking breakfast at a coffee house, perhaps Sheyler's in Orange Grove or the Parade Coffee House, now the Huntsman Pub. Alternatively they might turn into North Parade Passage, called Lilliput Alley in their day, to visit Sally Lunn's house. She made rolls for the pleasure grounds called Spring Gardens across the river. Late morning would see visitors thronging into the Abbey, perhaps in sedan chairs, while the afternoon would see them meeting friends as they strolled along the Parades. In the evening they would return, dressed in their finery, to go to the Assembly Rooms that once stood next to Parade Gardens.

After 1776, guests of the City Council might be invited to dine in the new Guildhall, designed by Thomas Baldwin, which replaced the old market hall. Today we can still admire the neo-classical splendour of the banqueting room, with its three magnificent chandeliers.

The Great Western Railway arrived in 1840. Designed by Isambard K. Brunel the trains ran on broad gauge track.

WALK OVERVIEW:	See guide to The Walks on page ####
Burton Street	Abbey Green
New Bond Street	Abbeygate Street
Northgate Street & High Street	Swallow Street
Guildhall (9)	**Abbey Church Yard & Bath Abbey (2)**
Orange Grove (15)	**Roman Baths (21) & Pump Room (18)**
Terrace Walk	Union Passage
N. Parade Passage & Sally Lunn's (N)	Upper Borough Walls

Chapter Seven

BATH ABBEY

The first Abbey on the site was founded in 676 when the Abbess Bertana established a house of nuns.

In 757 King Offa of Mercia replaced the nuns with the brothers of Saint Peter. The Abbey was described as being of wonderful workmanship – mira fabrica. Almost certainly they had used many of the carved stones from the ruined Roman city.

The first King of All England, Edgar, was crowned in Bath in 973 AD. Officiating at the ceremony were St. Dunstan, Archbishop of Canterbury, and Oswald, Archbishop of York.

St. Dunstan can be seen on the Victorian reredos. He carries a pair of pincers because he was once a blacksmith. The Devil, dressed as a woman, tried to tempt him but St Dunstan, noticing the cloven hoofs beneath the skirts, seized the devil's nose in his red-hot pincers.

After the Norman Conquest, the first French bishop was John of Tours. He had the old Saxon Abbey

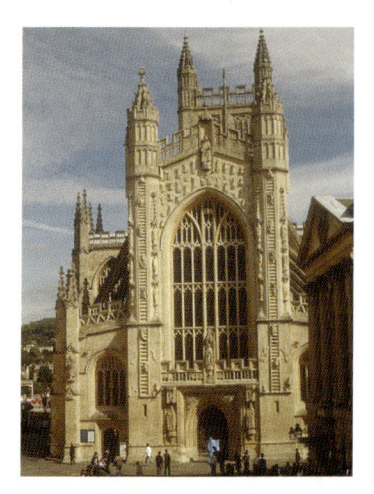

Chapter Seven

pulled down and replaced with a huge cathedral over 100 metres long.

The French Benedictine monks were said to have introduced weaving skills to the area.

By 1499, following fire, civil war and the Black Death, the number of monks was much reduced and the great church was in ruins. The new bishop, Oliver King, saw this decay and, worrying one night about it, he dreamt he saw angels in heaven, and other angels ascending and descending a ladder. A voice spoke, and said: Let an olive establish the crown and a king restore the Church. As his name was Oliver King, he assumed that this meant him, and he decreed that the church should be rebuilt, with his dream carved on the front. The descending angels, however, are coming down head first.

Sold during the Dissolution of the Monasteries, by the time of Elizabeth I the Abbey was an unfinished ruin. Elizabeth was so horrified when she saw it, she held a collection throughout England for it to be completed. She also said that henceforth it would be the city's parish church. It is often called the Lantern of the West.

Chapter Seven

THE GUILDHALL

By the mid-18th century the council decided they needed a new Guildhall, and a committee considered various proposals. Curiously, the plan by Thomas Atwood, a builder but also a councillor and the City Architect, kept being chosen. This was despite excellent plans being put forward by other architects. Eventually, however, Thomas Atwood fell through a floor while inspecting another building project, and his successor and protégé, Thomas Baldwin, finally produced the Guildhall we see today.

The Banqueting Room in the Guildhall is described as Bath's most beautiful room. In the Neo-classical style and painted in greens and gold, its walls are lined with portraits of the great and good.

Lighting is provided by three beautiful chandeliers. Made in London by Mr Parker, they cost £266 for all three: they are now regarded as irreplaceable.

At the back of the Guildhall is Bath Market. This area was first covered in the 1770s but was remodelled in the 1890s. Some of the little shops built at that time can still be seen in the interior and it still has the decorative iron pillars with flowers at their tops.

The wings to the Guildhall were built in 1896, designed by a Scottish architect, John Brydon. On the north side was the technical college and on the south other various civic offices and courts.

Chapter Seven

In order to construct the City Science, Art and Technical College, the White Lion Inn was pulled down, although it had been there throughout the 18th century.

The Victoria Library and Art Gallery (below) was added four years later. The library having moved to modern premises, the building now has three galleries. It has a fine collection of old Bath prints and paintings, including some by Gainsborough, Thomas Barker of Bath and Rowlandson.

The final Victorian building in this block, just scraping into her reign, is the Empire Hotel. The Empire, with its skyline representing a castle, a manor house and a cottage, dominates this part of the Bath skyline (below). Sometimes called Major Davis's Revenge, the city engineer built it after being cheated by the council out of designing the extension to the Pump Room. This was despite his plan being far superior as it protected the Roman Baths.

Chapter Seven - The Walk

THE WALK
Places to discover on the Chapter Seven Walk

Sally Lunn's house (1), along with the others in this row, is one of the oldest in Bath dating from 1620. The ground was sold for building after the dissolution of the monasteries .

Sally Lunn was a pastry cook who seems to have been active about 1770, although many legends have been attached to her. Her famous buns were originally called Spring Garden Rolls, and she baked them for the pleasure gardens that stood on the other side of the river.

The cellar was once the ground floor. The ground level was raised after John Wood had built the Parades and Gallaway had built his buildings.

Abbey Green (2): Many of these houses are a similar date to Sally Lunn's House. Some were refronted in the 18th century to make them look more modern. No. 3 has a timber-framed wall at the back.

The Crystal Palace was once a lodging attached to a coaching inn called The Three Tuns. The inn has vanished, and the pub was renamed in 1851.

The fish restaurant just outside Abbey Green was once an inn. First called the Raven, it was also known as the Druid's Head, Bladud's Head, The Talbot and Raven, and finally the Freemason's Tavern.

Chapter Seven - The Walk

Facing into the **Abbey Church Yard** is Marshal Wade's House (3), now the National Trust shop, with a holiday flat above it. Marshal Wade was MP for Bath in the 1720s.

Once the way out of the churchyard was nearly blocked at the Abbey end, with buildings right up against the walls on both sides. Marshal Wade had a wider passageway made into the High Street, but it was not until the 19th century when all the houses were finally removed.

In the northwest corner of the area was once another church called St Mary de Staules. When Elizabeth I made the Abbey the city's parish church, many of the old inner city churches were no longer needed. St Mary de Staules became a military hospital and prison during the Puritan occupation of the city and finally fell down in 1659.

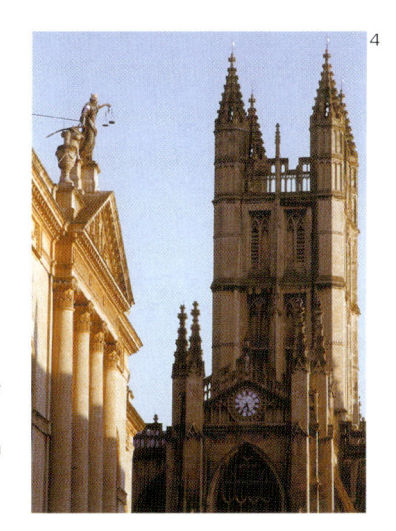

High Street (4) was once called the Market Place. In the centre stood the market hall, the pillory, and one of the conduits from which people collected their water.

The only water supply in the area now is a drinking fountain erected by Bath Temperance Association in 1861. It shows the figure of Rebecca at the Well and bears the inscription "Water is Best."

Chapter Seven - Sidetracks

Parade Gardens (6). Today the gardens, especially during the summer, are a popular resort for locals and visitors alike. It is noted for its colourful floral displays. There is a modern statue of Mozart (5), as well the remnants of the old mill that once stood beside the river.

In the 18th century before Pulteney Bridge was built a ferry would carry visitors over to Spring Gardens where the sports ground (the Rec) now stands. Wood (the Elder) raised his buildings at North Parade five metres to overcome the drainage problems. The area still floods to this day.

Chapter Seven - Sidetracks

Northumberland Passage (7 & 8) was built sometime before 1735, when it is shown on John Wood's Map. Known initially as Marchant's Court, it was named after the developer, a Quaker called Richard Marchant. This area is a maze of small alleys and lanes dedicated to shopping. The Corridor is a gated precinct resembling Burlington Arcade in London. Opposite you will find the entrance to the Guildhall Market which is well worth a visit. If you walk through you will come out near Pulteney Bridge and Parade Gardens (see opposite).

Royal warrants are numerous in Bath. The one left is in Northumberland Passage but there is one above the chemists in Argyle Street and another above the theatre in Beaufort Sq.

South Parade (9). At the end of South Parade was a ferry that would take visitors across to the fields of Bathwick or the shady groves of Widcombe and Lyncombe.

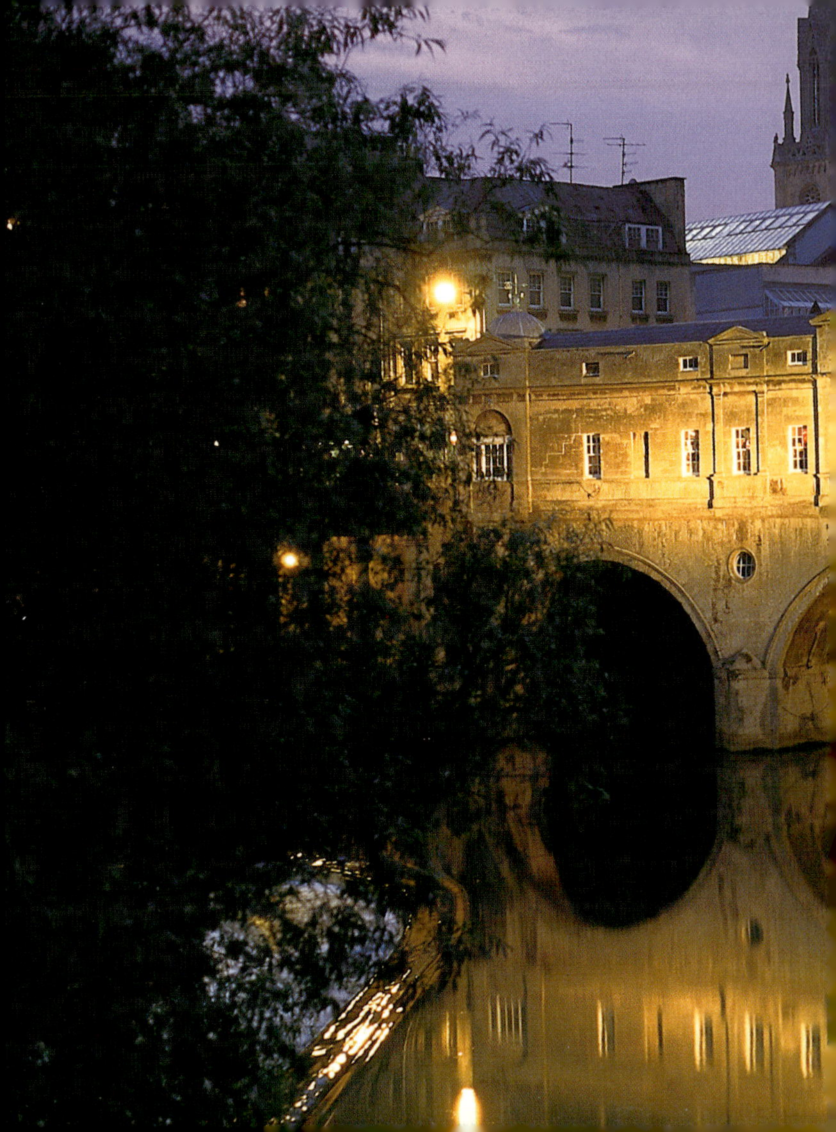

Pulteney Bridge
A taste of Italy

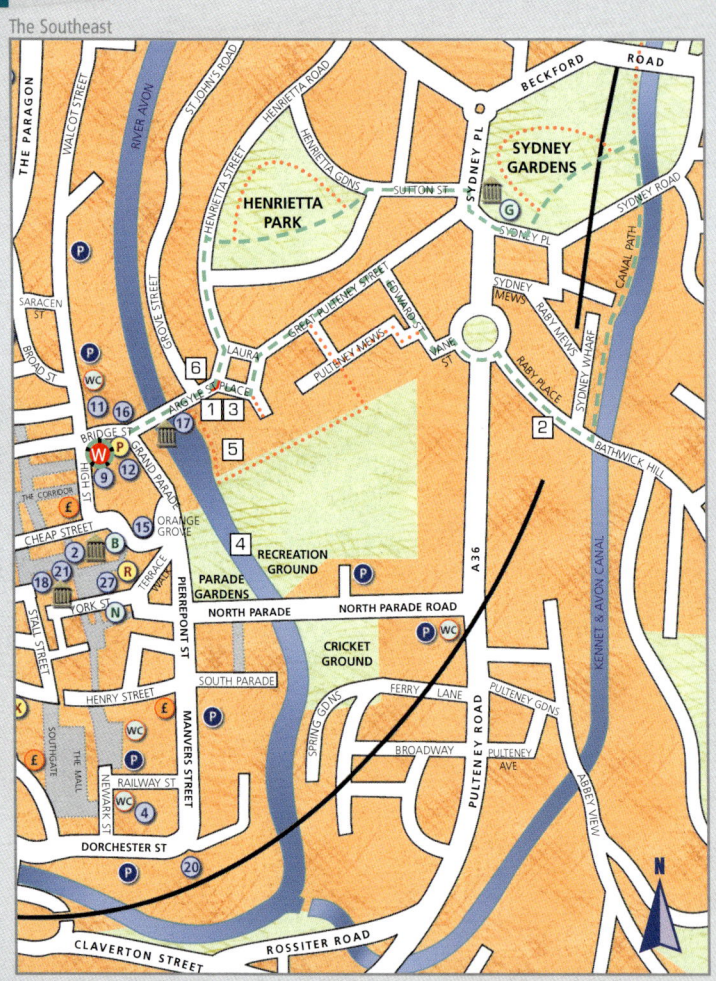

/ Chapter Eight

The Southeast

92

Chapter Eight - Introduction

Robert Adam's charming little Pulteney Bridge leads us across the River Avon into the Pulteney Estate. Here there were meant to be further squares and crescents, reached by streets leading off the magnificent Great Pulteney Street. Sadly, war with France and inflation meant this vision never came about, but we are left with open spaces such as the Recreation Ground and Henrietta Park. At the far end of the street can be seen the Holburne, now a fine arts museum but once the entrance to Sydney Gardens Vauxhall, a pleasure garden where there were breakfasts in the morning, concerts during the day and fireworks at night.

Beside the first shop on the bridge, steps lead down to the riverbank, from where can be seen the intimidating bulk of the Empire Hotel, with its curious skyline, and the Parade Gardens, which in summer is bright with flowers and colourful deckchairs. A walk beside the Avon will bring one to North Parade Bridge, from where there is a fine view of Pulteney Bridge, with its backdrop of Georgian terraces climbing the northern slopes.

Continuing onwards, the visitor reaches the Kennet and Avon Canal, completed in 1810. A walk along its towpath will lead your footsteps past the Widcombe flight of locks, past colourful narrowboats, and into Sydney Gardens. The enthusiastic walker can follow this path all the way to Reading and hence along the Thames to London, but that means leaving behind the Beauty of Bath.

WALK OVERVIEW:

Pulteney Bridge (17)	**Holburne Museum of Art (G)**
Argyle Street	Sydney Gardens
Laura Place	Canal Path
Henrietta Street	Bathwick Hill
Henrietta Park	Vane Street
Sutton Street	Edward Street
Sydney Place	Great Pulteney Street

Chapter Eight

PULTENEY BRIDGE

Designed by Robert Adam in 1768, work began a year later. It is thought to be based on Andrea Palladio's plan for the Rialto Bridge in Venice.

The first architect Pulteney consulted was Timothy Lightoler. His estimate of the cost was £1000. The final cost, however, was £11,500.

Because it is lined with shops, the bridge is sometimes compared with the Ponte Vecchio in Florence. The West end has been considerably altered.

The council did not like the design. They said the road was too narrow, and it would become congested with traffic and hence polluted. It was a remarkably prophetic announcement. However, they were not quite correct when they said that such a narrow bridge would never be considered elegant.

Chapter Eight

By the 1790s the bridge was beginning to collapse, and a temporary bridge had to be built. After rejecting a plan to demolish the bridge altogether, or add an extra one, just the north side was removed. Thus only the downstream side is actually by Robert Adam. The upstream side was designed 30 years later by the Bath architect John Pinch.

Over the years the shopkeepers, finding the shops too small, added the wooden "penthouses" which overhung the river on both sides. Eventually these were removed from the downstream view, but they still cling to the northern side of the bridge.

The bridge is now a National Monument.

Before the bridge was built, a ferry used to take people to the other side.

Below the bridge is the weir. Unlike the modern elliptical weir, which is part of the flood prevention scheme, the old one ran diagonally across the river, with a mill at each end. On the city side was the Monks' Mill, a tiny piece of which remains in Parade Gardens, and on the other side was Bathwick Mill. The flood gates at the Eastern end of the weir were built in 1972. The dry dock is now redundant but is a duck refuge.

Chapter Eight

SYDNEY GARDENS

In the early 1790s a scheme was put forward to develop some pleasure gardens on the hexagonal plot that was to be the centrepiece of the Pulteney Estate. It was intended to resemble the famous gardens in London at Vauxhall, and was to be called Sydney Gardens Vauxhall. The first tree was planted in 1793. The gardens opened on 11th May 1795.

A year later the hotel, or entrance to the gardens opened. Today we know it as the Holburne Museum. The building was intended to provide a grand closing vista to Great Pulteney Street.

Plans were drawn by Thomas Baldwin showing villa-like entrances at various points around the gardens. There was also intended to be an obelisk in front of the "Hotel". Unfortunately Baldwin went bankrupt and the surveyor-turned-architect Harcourt Masters took over. Baldwin's delightful, airy, design for the building was abandoned, and Masters produced almost the frontage we see today. The attic floor was added by John Pinch in 1836.

Sydney House, as it was known, became an hotel, with apartments for distinguished visitors. By 1842 it had become a hydropathic establishment.

Chapter Eight

It then became a school, Sydney College, before standing empty and almost derelict. Fortunately in 1915 it was purchased by the trustees of the Holburne of Menstrie collection, who employed Reginald Blomfield to create a gallery for them. Behind the old façade he built an entirely new museum, which today contains many fine paintings and objets d'art.

The gardens were encircled by a ride which had a Macadamised surface. This was not the tarmac that we know today, but a road made of layers of increasingly fine gravel. The ride also had leaping bars "and a shelter should the weather prove suddenly unfavourable."

Among other follies was a make-believe ruined castle – "the facsimile of those ancient Baronial towers that served as strongholds for the heroes of olden times" as the guidebook of 1825 describes it.

Swings were a popular feature of gardens at this time, and Sydney Gardens had several. Doctor Carmichael Smith had written a pamphlet entitled The Utility of Swinging in Pulmonary Consumption and other Disorders. No swinging was allowed on Sundays however.

In 1909 a copy of the portico to the Roman Temple was added as a memorial to the Bath Pageant.

The gardens were Jane Austen's favourite part of Bath. Here she could come to public breakfasts and evening concerts. She said that she would enjoy a concert there, for "the gardens are large enough for me to get pretty well beyond the reach of its sound." Possibly this was because the musicians were not always of the highest order!

Chapter Eight - The Walk

THE WALK
Places to discover on the Chapter Eight Walk

Faced with linking Adam's narrow bridge of shops to the far wider Great Pulteney Street, Baldwin introduced **Argyle Street**, its width somewhere between the two. It was not a happy solution, but perhaps the best in the circumstances.

The street contains some attractive shops. Chief among them is the chemist's shop (1) that dates from the 1820s. It still has the old bottles and jars that were the symbols of a chemist's. It also has above it the coat of arms of Queen Charlotte, made out of Coade Stone.

Dominating the street is the Argyle Chapel. It was designed in 1789 by Thomas Baldwin for a Nonconformist sect who had seceded from the Countess of Huntingdon's Connection. They paid him £4.

It became so fashionable that by 1821 they needed more accommodation, and Henry Goodridge produced the design we see today.

Great Pulteney Street: This magnificent street, designed by Thomas Baldwin, is 100 feet wide and 1000 feet long. Another one just like it was planned on the other side of Sydney Gardens, but the money ran out before the estate was finished.

Many famous (and infamous) people lived or lodged in this English boulevard. Among them are Mrs Fitzherbert, William Wilberforce, Napoleon III, William

Chapter Eight - The Walk

"Strata" Smith, Louis XVIII of France, Hannah More and Lola Montez.

Among the fictional lodgers is Catherine Morland, heroine of Jane Austen's novel Northanger Abbey, who lodges here with her benefactors, Mr and Mrs Allen.

Before the building of the Pulteney Estate, **Bath Wick** was a separate village, with its own church. There was, however, no bridge across the river.

As Bath Wick became gentrified, it was decided that the village church was unsuitable, and St Mary's Church was built at the foot of Bathwick Hill (2). The architect, John Pinch, used the newly fashionable Gothic style. It was consecrated in 1820, having cost more than £14,000.

In 1861 the old parish church, virtually ruinous, was replaced by St John's. However, it was too small and in 1869 an entirely new nave was added, dwarfing the previous church. Meanwhile remnants of the old parish church were used to construct the mortuary chapel in Bathwick cemetery.

Chapter Eight - Sidetracks

Sign in The Pulteney Arms pub (3) near Henrietta Gardens. This park which can be approached from Great Pulteney Street or Henrietta Street is very peaceful and has a special area set aside as a perfumed garden. This area of Bathwick was to be the site of a spectacular development with Henrietta Street leading to the centre piece of Frances Square. The French Revolution however stopped this.

North Parade Bridge (4) as seen from Pulteney Bridge. North Parade Bridge was built in 1836 by William Tierney Clarke.

Chapter Eight - Sidetracks

Where the recreation ground is now, there was a set of pleasure gardens called Spring Gardens. Here visitors to Bath could come to stroll in its walks, and to take its famous breakfasts. There were also firework displays and concerts. The Children's maze (5) was donated to the city by the builders Beazer. It is recommended that you walk from here along the river to the village of Widcombe and the Ring O Bells.

Grove Street (6) was at first known as Cheapside. This was one of the first streets to be built after Pulteney Bridge was built.

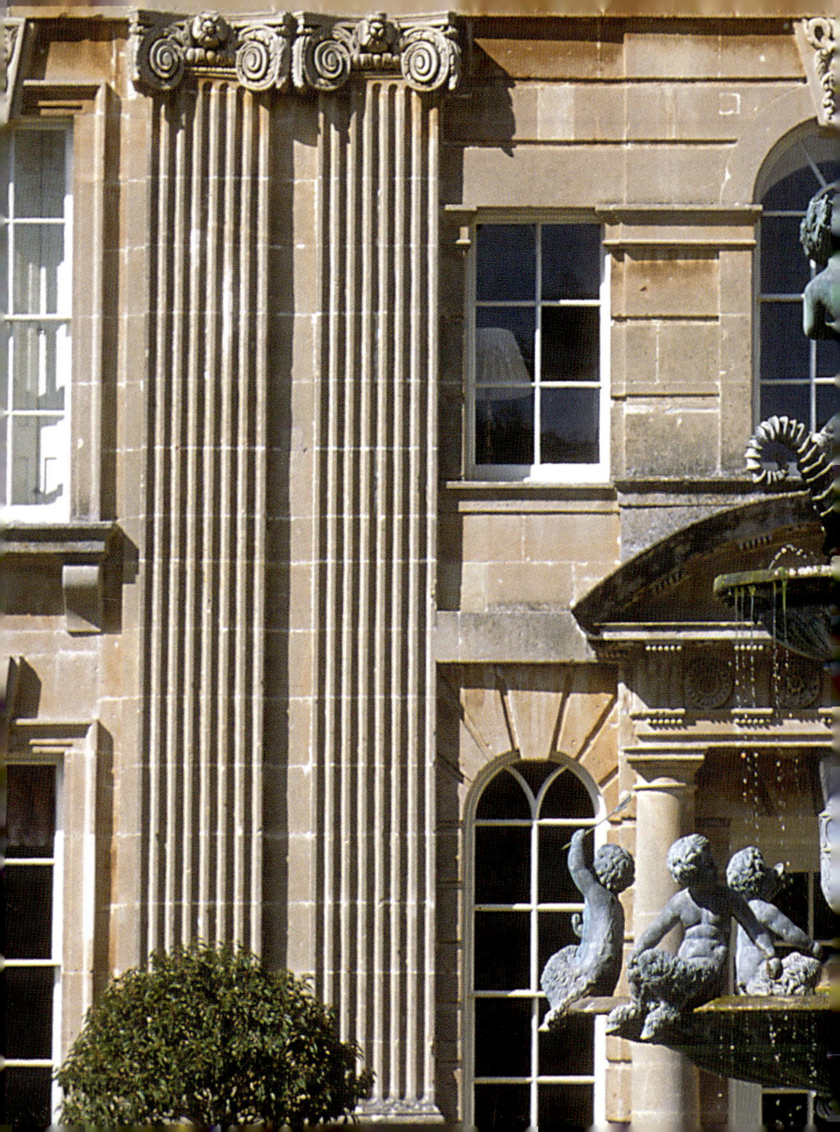

Widcombe Manor
Hidden Jewel

Chapter Nine

The Region

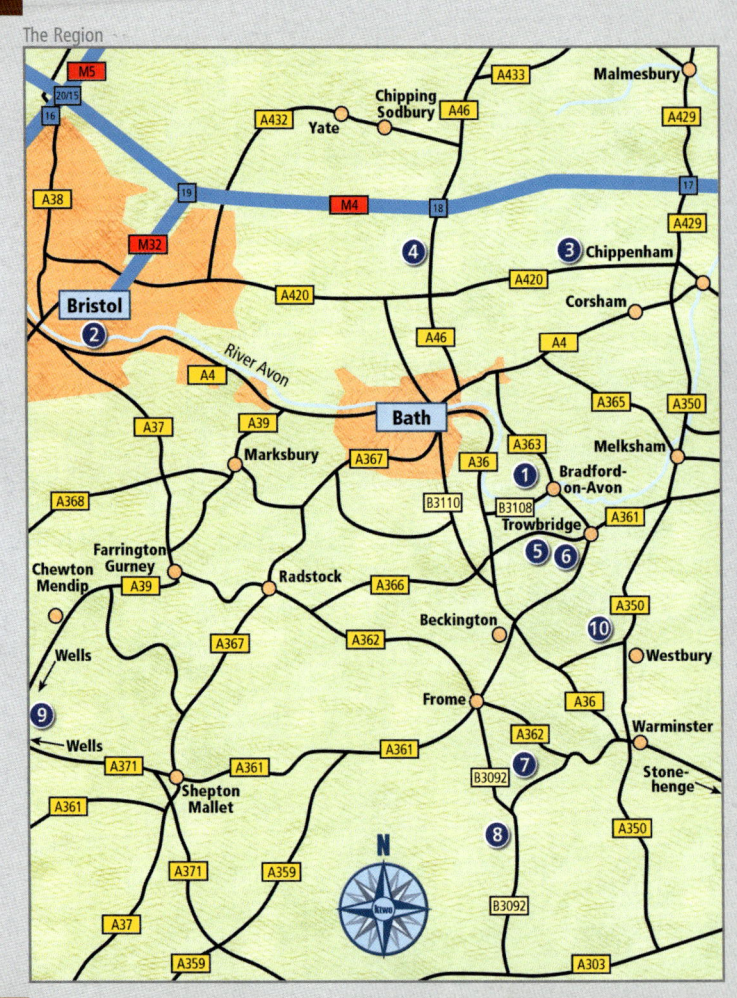

Chapter Nine - Introduction

Bath lies in an area of outstanding natural beauty and has a rich, varied heritage going back literally thousands of years. Travel in almost any direction through the stunning scenery of Somerset, Gloucestershire or Wiltshire and you will discover world class historical treasures.

Some of the most idyllic and unspoilt rural landscape in England for instance is found just to the north of Bath in the Cotswolds. Here you will find the villages of Stowe, Bourton on the Water and Chipping Camden nestling in the hills and creating picturesque scenes beloved of artists and photographers. To the East lie the rolling chalk downlands of Wiltshire and the ancient magical sites of Stonehenge, Avebury and the mysterious White Horses. To the South of Bath you will discover, amongst other wonderful sights, the ancient City of Wells and the alleged resting place of King Arthur at Glastonbury.

There is so much to see and do in this area that it is only possible to briefly highlight the very best. For heritage and indoor attractions, Lacock, Stourhead, Tytesfield, Bowood and Montacute are all magnificent. If you like gardens visit Corsham, Westonbirt, Iford, Lacock, Painswick and Stourhead. For those of you who like walking and have the energy the area is blessed with literally thousands of miles of marked and unmarked tracks and roads. Two famous walks are the Cotswold Way from Bath to Chipping Camden and the West Mendip Way from Weston-Super-Mare to Wells. Wiltshire alone has over 7,500 paths and The Ridgeway is allegedly the oldest path in Europe. For cyclists there is the 92 mile way-marked Avon Cycleway or the themed cycle routes in The Cotswolds like the Romantic Rivers route.

Bristol is Bath's big brother lying as it does just a few miles to the West. Over the last few years it has suddenly grown up and become rather cool with its harbourside cafes and arty culture. A visit to Bristol Zoo, The Empire Museum, SS Great Britain and the @Bristol museum with its Imax cinema and Wildwalk Rainforest are highly recommended - the train trip from Bath Spa only takes 15 minutes. NCM.

Chapter Nine - Northern Fringes

The river - seen here at Newbridge (right) - has been navigable from Bristol to Bath since 1727. Until 1812 there was no horse-towing path and boats were hauled by teams of men. The Avon cycle path starts at Bath and can be taken all the way to Bristol. The Sustrans cycle route links up and is an energetic way of travelling to Padstow.

Bathampton Toll Bridge from the Mill Hotel (right). The bridge was built in 1872 costing £4000. The toll is 50p. The George pub in Bathampton (below) has been a monastery, a morgue, a coaching house and a farm.

Chapter Nine - Northern Fringes

The City's Gas Works (left) were built when Bath's streets became gas lit in 1819. The first two gasometers were a tourist attraction. Pierce Egan, in his Walks Around Bath, designed a walk to take the curious out to see them. They are of course now empty but are a listed building.

The parish of St Mary the Virgin, Charlcombe, goes back to Anglo-Saxon times, although the church is Norman with a Norman font. The holy well in the garden (far left) is fed by an ancient spring in the Old Rectory garden, and the water is still used for baptisms. At the Batheaston Toll-Bridge (near left), the original list of tolls may still be seen.

Erected in 1892 at the cost of £200 the Iron Mission Chapel (left) at Bailbrook was built nearly 40 years after the Vicar of Batheaston thought that the lack of a chapel in Bailbrook was causing the locals to be "an unsatisfactory and disorderly set who congregated in the lanes and fields to gamble or create disturbances."

Chapter Nine - Southern Fringes

Prior Park (right) was built for Ralph Allen in 1735 by John Wood the Elder and was described by Pevsner as "the most ambitious and the most complete re-creation of Palladio's villas on English soil." The Palladian Bridge at Prior Park (above) was built in the 1750s and was based on a drawing by Palladio,

Widcombe Manor and Church (far right). The Manor was built for Philip Bennett, who married the daughter of Scarborough Chapman. The building is usually dated at about 1727, although it may be older. The architect is unknown.

Bath Abbey Cemetery (right) was designed by the great gardener, architect and reformer, John Claudius Loudon. His concern about the lack of scientific principles in managing burial grounds drove him on with the project despite ill-health. He died in 1843. The cemetery was consecrated in the following year.

Chapter Nine - Southern Fringes

Sham Castle (left). A folly built in 1762 by Ralph Allen as an eyecatcher to enrich the view from the city. It can be seen from Grand Parade and is floodlit at night.

A farmhouse in Smallcombe (left) viewed from the National Trust's Skyline Walk which offers fine views of the city and surrounding hills. This unique walk retains an 18th century atmosphere and largely contributes to Bath's World Heritage Site status

With the intimidating polar bear fishing for passers-by, it is tempting to think that Bear Flat (left) is named after the inn, but in fact the name has more to do with barley. Widcombe in the snow (below).

Chapter Nine - Beyond Bath

PLACES TO VISIT IN THE BATH VICINITY
(with map reference number, distance and direction from Bath)

Avebury   27m E
Stone circle site
Bowood House   20m ENE
Stately home, gardens and adventure playground.
Bradford-on-Avon (1)   8m ESE
Village on river, with medieval Tithe Barn.
Bristol (2)   15m NW
Large city with airport, museums, tourist attractions, zoo, entertainment & sporting venues.
Castle Combe (3)   14m NE
Idyllic English village.
Cheddar Gorge & Caves 30m WSW
Dramatic geological formations
Cirencester   35m NE
Old Roman town of Corinium
Dyrham Park (4)   6m N
Stately home, gardens and park. National Trust (NT)
Farleigh Castle (5)   9m SE
Castle ruins and medieval church.
Glastonbury   33m SW
Tor and historic town
Iford Manor (6)   10m SE
Award winning gardens

Clifton Suspension Bridge, Bristol

Castle Combe

Dyrham Park

Iford Manor

Stonehenge

Chapter Nine - Beyond Bath

Glastonbury Tor

Wells Cathedral

Longleat Estate (7)   18m SSE
Stately home, safari and theme park
Salisbury   40m SE
Cathedral and historic town
Stonehenge   38m SE
Famous ancient stone circle
Stourhead (8)   15m S
Stately home and grounds. NT
Wells (9)   20m SW
Cathedral and historic city
Westbury (10)   18m SE
White Horse
Wookey Hole Caves   25m SW
Famous caves

Westbury White Horse

Wookey Hole Caves

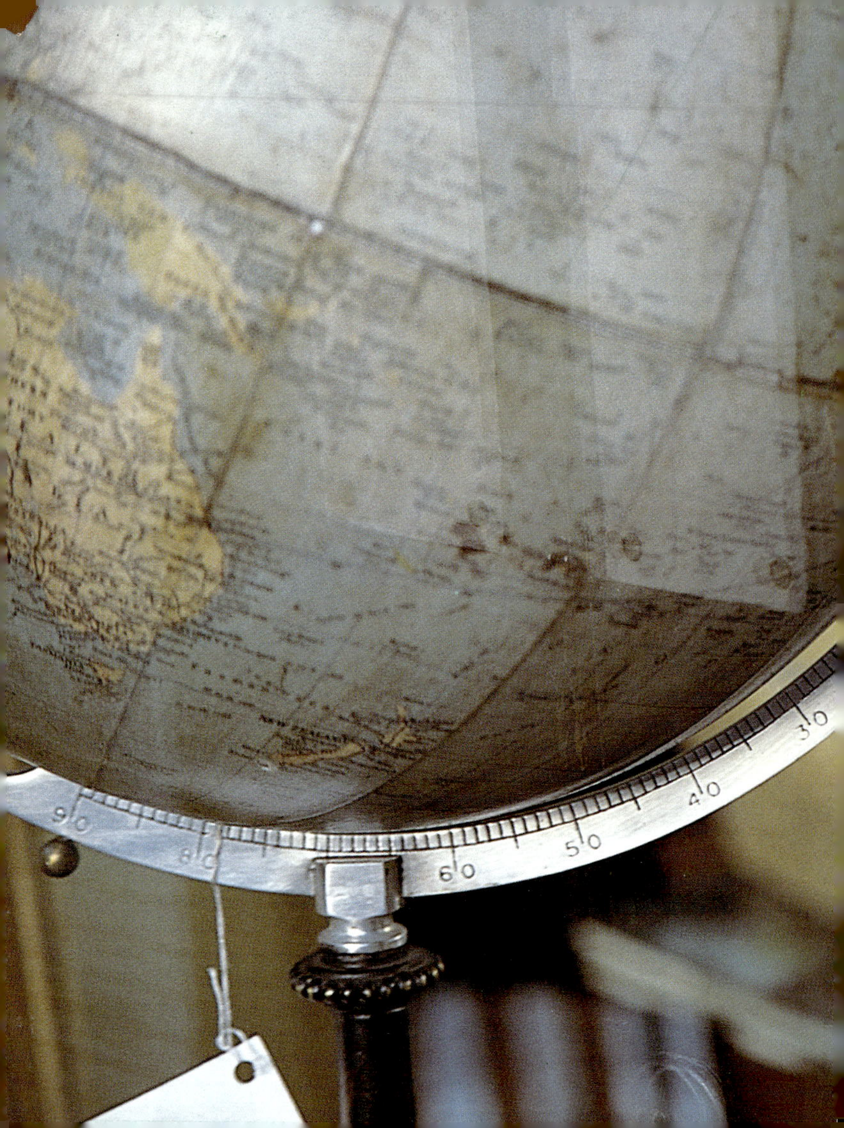
90
80
60
50
40
30

The Listings
Find It Here

Bath's Shopping Highway

> Bath's Shopping Highway

For more info. visit www.finditbath.co.uk

The pedestrian-friendly shopping streets that stretch in a straight line from the North end of Milsom St. to the Southern end of Southgate form Bath's spine. The following few pages start at the top of Milsom St. and move southward listing all relevant establishments along the way. Many businesses in Bath have links from Find It Bath, "Bath's best website."

Colour Codes for Categories

- ◯ Books
- ● Clothing/Shoes/Accessories
- ● Department Store
- ● Food & Drink
- ○ Gifts
- ● House/Home
- ■ Jewellery
- ■ Miscellaneous
- ■ Newsagent
- ■ Pharmacy
- ■ Sports/Outdoor Outfitters
- ■ Stationery
- ☐ Technology/Entertainment
- ■ Toys
- ▲ Financial Services
- ▲ Hairdressers

*Six of the Best as voted on Find It Bath

Loch Fyne Fish Restaurant	750120	●
24 Milsom St.		
Litten Tree	310772	●
23 Milsom St.		
Blue	462111	●
25 Milsom St.		
Cargo Homeshop	466066	●
26/27 Milsom St.		
Moss Bros	461650	●
22 Milsom St.		
Sofa Workshop	442586	●
21 Milsom St.		
Jaeger	466415	●
20 Milsom St.		
Culpeper the Herbalist	425875	■
28 Milsom St.		
Vintage to Vogue	337323	●
28 Milsom St.		
Resort	465589	●
29 Milsom St.		
Austin Reed	464340	●
19 Milsom St.		
Gap Kids	483822	●
17 Milsom St.		
Britannia Building Society	463327	▲
30 Milsom St.		
Paperchase	446824	■
31 Milsom St.		
Bengal Brasserie	447906	●
32 Milsom St.		
Hobbs	465330	●
32 Milsom St.		

Bath's Shopping Highway

Duo Shoes of Bath	465533	**Emma Somerset**	466505
33 Milsom St.	🟢	46 Milsom St.	🟢
Bella Pasta	462368	**Lloyds Bank**	310256
15 Milsom St.	🟣	47 Milsom St.	🔺
Jolly's	462811	**Goldsmiths**	464721
14 Milsom St.	🔵	1 Milsom St.	🟥
Nitya		**Nationwide**	490200
34 Milsom St.	🟢	21 Old Bond St.	🔺
Gabucci	469975	**Gieves & Hawkes**	463839
35 Milsom St.	🟢	20 Old Bond St.	🟢
Barclays Bank	494000	**Gap**	463132
37 Milsom St.	🔺	18-19 Old Bond St.	🟢
Me2u	482020	**Jackpot**	329392
38 Milsom St.	🟪	1 New Bond St Bdgs	🟢
NatWest	0845 6101234		
39 Milsom St.	🔺		

For **Shires Yard** shopping area go left here

Pulteney Bridge Flowers	448429
Kiosk 1 Shire's Yard	🟧
Kaliko	420060
6 Milsom St.	🟢
Alliance & Leicester	446917
42 Milsom St.	🔺
Waterstones	448515
4-5 Milsom St.	🟡
HSBC	0845 7404404
45 Milsom St.	🔺
Maythers	443099
Milsom St.	🟡
East	
2 Milsom St.	🟢

Union Street

Bath's Shopping Highway

Toni & Guy	484284	**Starbucks**	443409
2 New Bond St Bdgs	🔺	13 Old Bond St.	🟣
Mobile Phones Direct	484865	**Cecil Gee**	483443
3 New Bond St Bdgs	⬜	8-10 Old Bond St.	🟢
Bloomsbury & Metropolitan	461049	**Lifestyle Pharmacy**	465576
15 New Bond St.	⚪	14 New Bond St.	🟩
Russell & Bromley	460951	**Justice**	
16-17 Old Bond St.	🟢	1 Burton St.	🟥
Hawkins Clinic	466011	**The Body Shop**	482289
15 Old Bond St.	🟧	2 Burton St.	🟧
Mallory	788800	**Kolor**	
5 Old Bond St.	🟥	3 Burton St.	⚪
Past Times	310410	**Woods**	445347
15 Old Bond St.	⚪	12 Old Bond St.	🟪
Clive Ranger	444980	**Christopher Barry**	464585
6-7 Old Bond St.	🟥	12a Old Bond St.	🟢
Shoon	480095	**Café Nero**	
14 Old Bond St.	🟢	Old Bond St.	🟣
		Devon Savouries	466290
		4a Burton St.	🟢
		Vodafone	484688
		5 Burton St.	⬜
		Lush	428271
		12 Union St.	⚪
		Dr China	
		13 Union St.	🟧
		Thorntons	465637
		14 Union St.	🟣
		H. Samuel	462407
		15 Union St.	🟥
		Next	469828
		16 Union St.	🟢

ktwo's Six of the Best* the Shopping Highway

1. Roman Baths (museum)
2. Metropolitan (café)
3. Waterstones (shop)
4. Gap (shop)
5. Bloomsbury's (shop)
6. Loch Fyne (restaurant)

Bath's Shopping Highway

Etam	466443
11 Union St.	🟢

For **The Corridor**
shopping area go left here

Tie Rack	464357
18 Union St.	🟢
Goldsmiths	462370
19 Union St.	🟥
Clarks Shoe Shop	462632
10 Union St.	🟢
The Disney Store	429853
9 Union St.	⬜
Carphone Warehouse	
Union St.	☐
WHSmiths	460522
6-7 Union St.	🟡 🟨 🟪 ☐ ⬜
Accessorize	422833
21 Union St.	🟢
Monsoon	463500
22 Union St.	🟢
Phones4u	482486
5 Union St.	☐
Cocoa House	444030
23 Union St.	🟣
Dune	422286
4 Union St.	🟢
Country Casuals	465289
3 Union St.	🟢
Dixons	484118
24 Union St.	☐

For **Westgate St. & Sawclose**
shopping areas, go right here

For **Cheap St.**
shopping area, go left here

The Roundhouse	425070
Stall St.	🟣
Gadget Shop	0800 7838343
44 Stall St.	○ ☐
Envy	330542
Stall St.	🟢
La Baguette	480833
3 Stall St.	🟣
Holland and Barrett	330812
Stall St.	🟣
Bateman's Optician	464365
6 Abbey Churchyard	🟧

For **Abbey Churchyard**
shopping area, go left here

Edinburgh Woollen Mill	463910
41 Stall St.	🟢
O2	443614
Stall St.	☐
Bhs	423527
38-39 Stall St.	🟢
The Roman Baths Shop	**477785**
Stall St.	○
The Officers Club	481128
Stall St.	🟢
Barratts Shoes	460424
34 Stall St.	🟢
Vodafone	481300
5 Stall St.	☐
Sunglass Hut	465304
6 Stall St.	🟢

Bath's Shopping Highway

Next	448251	**Starbucks**	316881
33 Stall St.	🟢	22 Stall St.	🟣
River Island	464895	**Evans**	466491
7 Stall St.	🟢	20 Stall St.	🟢
Ciro Citterio	464798	**Clinton Cards**	481763
32 Stall St.	🟢	Stall St.	🟪
Sole Trader	482040	**The Link**	337667
9 Stall St.	🟢	56 Southgate	⬜
Autonomy		**Bhs Home Store**	317387
30-31 Stall St.	🟢	1 Southgate	⚪
Whittards	428684	**Phones4u**	332047
10 Stall St.	🟣	Southgate	⬜
Ernest Jones	463215	**Vision Express**	313422
11 The Mall	🟧	53 Southgate	🟧
Thorntons	443250	**Top Shop**	461546
11 Stall St.	🟣	52 Southgate	🟢
Pilot	444909	**Currys**	466543
27 Stall St.	🟢	2 Southgate	⬜
Ann Summers		**Jessops**	331154
Stall St.	🟢	Southgate	⬜
HMV	466681	**Wallis**	462015
13-15 Stall St.	⬜	3 Southgate	🟢
Halifax	0845 6005510	**Mothercare**	466245
26 Stall St.	🔺	44 Southgate	🟧
Burton Menswear	447978	**Allsports**	425998
24 Stall St.	🟢	Southgate	🟦
Dorothy Perkins	448547	**GNC**	471093
24 Stall St.	🟢	5 Southgate	🟣
Marks & Spencer	462591	**Milletts**	429596
16 Stall St.	🔵	6 Southgate	🟦
Claires Accessories	332332	**Superdrug**	331338
25 Stall St.	🟢	42 Southgate	🟩

Bath's Shopping Highway / Cafés & Fast Food

Adams	463800
7 Southgate	🟢
HSBC	0845 7404404
Southgate	🔺
Bookworld	
9 Southgate	🟡
Booksale	464114
10 Southgate	🟡
The Card Market	421935
11 Southgate	🟪
McDonalds	463764
40 Southgate	🟣
Game	464164
12 Southgate	⬜

For **Marchants Passage** shopping area, go left here

Halifax	0845 600 5510
38 Southgate	🔺
Boots	464402
Southgate	🔵 🟩
Cooper & Tanner	
34 Southgate	🟧
Chopstick	425067
33 Southgate	🟣
Post Office	
32 Southgate	🟪
Toni & Guy	
31 Southgate	🔺
BCH Camping	460200
30 Southgate	🟦

Cafés & Fast Food

For more info. visit www.finditbath.co.uk

Adventure Café	462038
5 Princes Buildings, George St.	
Archway Café, The	463329
Arch 7 Lower Bristol Rd.	
Bath Bun Tea Room	462413
3 Lilliput Court, North Parade Passage	
Ben's Cookies	460983
21 Union Passage	
Binks Restaurant	466563
17-18 Cheap St.	
Bonghy-Bo Café Bar	462276
Barton Court, Upper Borough Walls	
Boston Tea Party	313901
Kingsmead Square	
Bridge Coffee Shop, The	483339
17 Pulteney Bridge	

Northumberland Passage

Cafés & Fast Food

Burger King	319169	**Garden Café**	446001
4 Cheap St.		9 Terrace Walk	
Café Nero		**Green Cat Café**	425193
11 Old Bond St.		18 Northumberland Place	
Café Nero		**Guildhall Market Café**	461593
21 High St.		Guildhall High St.	
Café Rene	447147	**Hardys of Wessex**	316796
Shires Yard		14a Westgate Buildings	
Café Retro	339347	**Holburne Museum Tea House**	420465
18 York St.		Great Pulteney St.	
Café Solo	466856	**Itchy Feet**	337987
7a Princes Building		4 Bartlett St.	
California Kitchen	471471	**Jazz Café**	**329002**
The Podium		**1 Kingsmead St., Kingsmead Square**	
Carwardine's	460088	**La Baguette**	
The Podium		Stall St.	
City Gourmet Ltd.	471555	**Le Petit Cochon**	**317204**
8 The Podium		**25 Claverton Bdgs, Widcombe Prd**	
Click Internet Café	**337711**		
Manvers St.			
Cocoa House	444030		
23 Union St.			
Coffee Mill, The	330441		
3 High St., Weston			
Costa Stores	483047		
44 Stall St.			
David Thayer	460434		
8 York St.			
Doolally's	444122		
51 Walcot St.			
Fodders Sandwich Bar	462165		
9 Cheap St.			

Ktwo's Six of the Best* Cafés & Fast Food

1. Adventure Café
2. Metropolitan
3. Café Retro
4. Shoon
5. Jazz Café
6. Waterstones Café

Cafés & Fast Food / Guest Houses

Les Munchies	480779
Kingsmead Square	
Living Stone Coffee Shop Ltd	332100
17 Livingstone Rd.	
McDonalds	463764
38-41 Southgate	
Metropolitan Café Ltd	482680
15 New Bond St.	
Phipps Bakery	462483
19-20 Kingsmead Square	
Pump Room	
Stall St.	
Ricki's Ltd	460314
Unit 13 The Mall, Southgate	
Riverside Café	480532
17 Argyle St.	
Rhythm & Beans	789996
36 Monmouth St.	
Sally Lunns Tea House	461634
4 North Parade Passage	
Same Time, Same Place	329999
Bartlett St. Antique Centre, Bartlett St.	
Schwartz Bros.	461726
Sawclose & Walcot St.	
Snack Café	461705
1 Railway St.	
Starbucks Coffee Co	443409
13 Old Bond St. & 22 Stall St.	
Subway	789958
11 Westgate St.	
Take 5	425888
1 Grove St.	
Trams Restaurant	466847
Bath Bus Station Manvers St.	
Waverly Café	462553
4 New St. West, Kingsmead Square	

Guest Houses

For more info. visit www.finditbath.co.uk

Aimee's Guest House	330133
6 Manvers St.	
Albany Guest House	313339
24 Crescent Gdns., Upper Bristol Rd.	
Alderney Guest House	312365
3 Pulteney Rd.	
Aquae Sulis Guest House	420061
176 Newbridge Rd.	
Armstrong House	442211
41 Crescent Gdns.	
Ashgrove Guest House	421911
39 Bathwick St.	
Ashley House	425027
8 Pulteney Gdns.	
Astor Guest House	429134
14 Oldfield Rd.	
Avon Guest House	313009
1 Pulteney Gdns.	
Badminton Villa Guest House	859090
10 Upper Oldfield Park	
Bailbrook Lodge	859090
35-37 London Rd. West	

Guest Houses

Beckford's	334959	**Highways House**	421238
59 Upper Oldfield Park		143 Wells Rd.	
Belmont, The	423082	**Holly Villa Guest House**	310331
Belmont, Lansdown		14 Pulteney Gdns.	
Brocks Guest House	338374		
32 Brock St.			
Crescent Guest House	425945		
21 Crescent Gdns.			
Daphne Strong	423434		
51 Wellsway			
Dene Villa	427676		
5 Newbridge Hill			
Devonshire House	312495		
143 Wellsway			
Dorset Villa B&B	425975		
14 Newbridge Rd.			
Elgin Villa B&B	424557		
6 Marlborough Lane			
Forres House	427698		
172 Newbridge Rd.			
Glan Y Dwr	317521	**Kinlet Guest House**	420268
14 Newbridge Hill		99 Wells Way	
Glen View	421376	**Koryu Guest House**	337642
162 Newbridge Rd.		7 Pulteney Gdns.	
Greenways	310132	**Lamp Post Villa**	331221
1 Forester Rd.		3 Crescent Gdns.	
Grove Lodge	310860	**Lavender House**	314500
11 Lambridge, London Rd.		17 Bloomfield Park	
Haydon House	444919	**Leighton House**	314769
9 Bloomfield Park		139 Wells Rd.	
Henry Guest House	424052	**Lindisfarne**	466342
6 Henry St.		41a Warminster Rd.	

Queensberry Hotel, Russel Street

Guest Houses / Hotels

Lynwood Guest House	426410
6 Pulteney Gdns.	
Mardon Guest House	311624
1 Pulteney Terrace	
Marisha's	446881
68 Newbridge Hill	
Marlborough House	318175
1 Marlborough Lane	
Milton House	335632
75 Wellsway	
Number 30	337393
Crescent Gdns.	
Oakleigh Guest House	315698
19 Upper Oldfield Park	
Old Red House B & B	330464
37 Newbridge Rd.	
Parkside	429444
11 Marlborough Lane	
Prior House	313587
3 Marlborough Lane	
Roman City Guest House	**463668**
18 Raby Place, Bathwick	
Royal Park Guest House	317651
16 Crescent Gdns.	
Thomas House	789540
3 Thomas St.	
Toad Hall Guest House	423254
6 Lime Grove, Bathwick	
Walton's Guest House	426528
17 Crescent Gdns.	
White Guest House	426075
23 Pulteney Gdns.	

Hotels

For more info. visit www.finditbath.co.uk

Abbey Hotel, The	461603
North Parade	
Apsley House Hotel	336966
Newbridge Hill	
Ashley Villa Hotel	421683
26 Newbridge Rd.	
Avondale Riverside Hotel	859946
London Rd. East, Bathford	
Ayrlington Hotel	425495
24-25 Pulteney Rd.	
Backpackers Hotel*	446787
13 Pierrepont St.	
Bath Lodge Hotel	723040
Norton St. Philip	
Bath Priory Hotel	331922
Weston Rd.	
Bath Spa Hotel	0870 4008222
Sydney Rd.	
Bath Tasburgh Hotel	425096
Warminster Rd.	
Brompton House Hotel	859847
St. Johns Rd., Bathwick	
Carfax Hotel	462089
Great Pulteney St.	
Cliffe Hotel	723226
Crow Hill, Limpley Stoke	
Combe Grove Manor Hotel	834644
Monkton Combe	

Hotels

Comfort Inn, The Henrietta St.	469151	**Lansdown Grove Hotel** Lansdown Rd.	483888
County Hotel, The **18-19 Pulteney Rd.**	**425003**	**Laura Place Hotel** 3 Laura Place	463815
Cranleigh 159 Newbridge Hill	310197	**Leigh Park Hotel** Leigh Rd. West, Bradford On Avon	868686
Dukes Hotel Great Pulteney St.	787960	**Limpley Stoke Hotel** Woods Hill, Limpley Stoke	723226
Eagle House Hotel Church St., Bathford	858476	**Lodge Hotel** Bathford	858467
Edgar Hotel, The 64 Great Pulteney St.	420619	**Menzies Waterside** Rossiter Rd.	338855
Express Holiday Inn Brougham Hayes	0870 4442792	**Oldfields Hotel** 102 Wells Rd.	317984
Forte Travelodge A36 Trowbridge Rd., Beckington	420972		
Fountain House 9-11 Fountain Bdgs, Lansdown Rd.	864885		
Francis Hotel Queen Square	0870 4008223		
Georges Hotel 2/3 South Parade	464923		
Harington's Hotel 8-10 Queen St.	461728		
Henrietta Hotel 32 Henrietta St.	447779		
Hilton Bath City Walcot St.	463411		
Hotel St Clair 1a Crescent Gdns.	425543		
Kennard Hotel 11 Henrietta St.	310472		

Francis Hotel, Queen Square

Hotels / Museums

Parade Park, The	463384
10 North Parade	
Pratts Hotel	460441
4-8 South Parade	
Pulteney Hotel	421261
14 Pulteney Rd.	
Queensberry Hotel	447928
Russel St.	
Royal Crescent Hotel	823333
16 Royal Crescent	
Royal Hotel	463134
52 Manvers St.	
St Christophers Inn*	**481444**
9 Green St.	
Ston Easton Park Hotel	01761 241631
Ston Easton, Near Bath	
Villa Magdala	466329
Henrietta Rd.	
Wentworth House	339193
106 Bloomfield Rd.	
White Hart Inn*	313985
Widcombe	
Windsor Hotel	**422100**
69 Great Pulteney St.	
YMCA*	460471
Broad St. Place	

*Hostel-style budget accommodation

Museums

For more info. visit www.finditbath.co.uk

American Museum & Gardens	460503	
Claverton Manor		A
Bath Abbey Heritage Vaults	422462	
Bath Abbey		B
Bath Royal Lit. & Sci. Inst.	312084	
Queen Square		C
Beckford's Tower & Museum	460705	
Lansdown		D
Building of Bath Museum	333895	
Paragon		F
Guildhall Banqueting Room	477724	
High St.		9
Holburne Museum of Art	466669	
Sydney Gdns		G

Ktwo's Six of the Best* Museums

1. American Museum
2. Museum of Costume
3. Roman Baths
4. Holburne Museum of Art
5. Victoria Art Gallery
6. Building of Bath Museum

Museums / Galleries / Restaurants

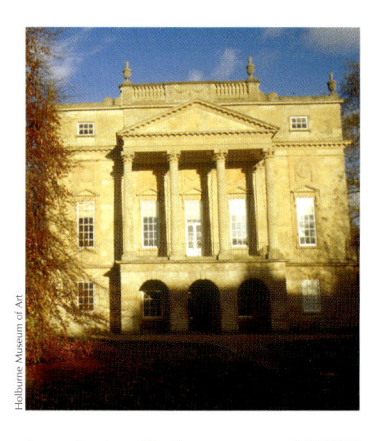

Holburne Museum of Art

Jane Austen Centre	443000
40 Gay St.	H
Museum of Bath at Work	318348
Julian Rd.	I
Museum of Costume	477752
Bennett St.	J
Museum of East Asian Art	464640
12 Bennett St.	K
No 1 Royal Crescent	428126
1 Royal Crescent	L
Postal Museum	460333
8 Broad St.	M
Roman Baths & Pump Room	477785
Abbey Church Yard	21
Sally Lunn's Refreshment House	461634
North Parade Passage	N
William Herschel Museum	311342
19 New King St.	O

Galleries

For more info. visit www.finditbath.co.uk

Beaux Arts	464850
12-13 York St.	R
Invention	421700
Lower Borough Walls	X
Rooksmoor Gallery	420495
31 Brock St.	T
Rostra Gallery	448121
5 George St.	S
Russell Rare Prints	466335
6 Margaret's Bdgs	U
Six Chapel Row	337900
6 Chapel Row	V
St James Gallery	319197
9 Margaret's Bdgs	W
Victoria Art Gallery	477233
Bridge St.	P

Restaurants

For more info. visit www.finditbath.co.uk

Arabesque	481333
The Podium	
ASK	489997
Broad St.	
Bathtub Bistro	460593
2 Grove St.	

Restaurants

Beaujolais Restaurant	423417	**Curry Mahal**	789666
5 Chapel Row		31 Belvedere, Lansdown Rd.	
Bella Pasta	462368	**Demuth's Restaurant**	446059
15 Milsom St.		2 North Parade Passage	
Bengal Brasserie	447906	**Eastern Eye**	422323
32 Milsom St.		8a Quiet St.	
Bottelino's	464861	**F.east**	333500
5 Bladud Buildings, Roman Rd.		27 High St.	
Browns	461199	**Firehouse Rotisserie**	482070
Orange Grove		2 John St.	
Caffe Martini	460818	**Fishworks**	448707
George St.		6 Green St.	
Caffe Uno	461140	**Garfunkels**	461465
The Empire, Grand Parade		Orange Grove	
Circus Restaurant	318918	**Green Park Brasserie**	338565
34 Brock St.		Green Park Station	
Clarkes	444440	**Hands Restaurant**	**463928**
7 Argyle St.		**9 York St.**	
		Hole in the Wall, The	425242
		16 George St.	
		La Flamenca	463626
		12a North Parade (Vaults)	
		Lambrettas Bistro Bar	464650
		8-10 North Parade	
		Las Iguanas	336666
		Seven Dials	
		Loch Fyne Restaurant	750120
		24 Milsom St.	
		Maharaja	484931
		14 North Parade	
		Moody Goose Restaurant	466688
		7a Kingsmead Square	

Ktwo's Six of the Best* Restaurants

1. Olive Tree
2. Fishworks
3. Moon & Sixpence
4. Firehouse
5. Yum Yum Thai
6. Loch Fyne

Restaurants

Moon & Sixpence	460962	**Shangri-La Restaurant**	338200
6a Broad St.		2 George St.	
No. 10 Restaurant	333939	**Thai Balcony**	444450
10 Upper Borough Walls		Seven Dials, Sawclose	
No. 5 Bistro	**444499**	**The Francis on the Square**	424257
5 Argyle St.		Queen Square	
Ocean Pearl	331238	**Vaults Restaurant**	442265
The Podium		Sawclose	
Old Orleans	333233	**Walrus & The Carpenter**	314864
1 St. Andrews Terrace, Bartlett St.		28 Barton St.	
Olive Tree	447928	**Wife of Bath**	461745
Russell St.		12 Pierrepont St.	
Pasta Galore	463861	**Woods Restaurant**	314812
31 Barton St.		9 Alfred St.	
Pastiche Bistro	442323	**Yak Yeti Yak**	422100
16 Argyle St.		12 Argyle St.	
Peking Chinese Restaurant	466377	**Yum Yum Thai**	445253
1-2 New St., Kingsmead Square		17 Kingsmead Sq.	
Pinch of Salt	**421251**		
11 Margaret's Buildings			
Pizza Express	420119		
1 Barton St.			
Popjoys	460494		
Beau Nash House, Sawclose			
Rajpoot Tandoori	466833		
4 Argyle St.			
Raphael	480042		
Upper Borough Walls			
Sands Restaurant	443900		
7 Edgar Buildings			
Seafood Café	448707		
6 Green St.			

Pinch of Salt Restaurant, Margaret's Buildings

Retailers

Retailers

For more info. visit www.finditbath.co.uk

Colour Codes for Categories

- 🔴 Antiques
- 🟠 Art
- 🟡 Books
- 🟢 Clothing/Shoes/Accessories
- 🔵 Department Store
- 🟣 Food & Drink
- ⚪ Gifts
- ⚫ House/Home
- 🟥 Jewellery
- 🟧 Miscellaneous
- 🟨 Newsagent
- 🟩 Pharmacy
- 🟦 Sports/Outdoor Outfitters
- 🟪 Stationery
- ⬜ Technology/Entertainment
- 🔲 Toys

Abbey Photo Service	480541
9 York St.	⬜
Ace Camera & Optics	466975
16 Green St.	⬜
Aga Shop	335237
12 Widcombe Parade	⚫
Alexandra May	465094
23 Brock St.	○
An Affair with Wood	460808
Stall 22-25, Guildhall Market	⚫
Animal	448934
14-16 The Corridor	🟢
Ann King	336245
38 Belvedere, Lansdown Rd.	🟢
Ann le Coz	463938
26a Belvedere Lansdown Rd.	⚫
Antique Map Shop	446097
Pulteney Bridge	🔴
Antique Textiles	310795
34 Belvedere, Lansdown Rd.	🔴
Antiques & Interior Decoration	
12 Queen St	🔴
Antoni's Jewellers	447551
5 Northumberland Place	🟥
Apoidea	462176
Broad St. Place	🟥
Aqua Leisure	446681
5 Abbey Gate	🟦
Arcania	335223
17 Union Passage	🟧
Argos	462762
3 Marchants Passage	🔵
Arlington Interiors	420999
2 Mile End, London Rd.	⚫
Art of Bath	482748
80 Walcot St.	⬜
Assembly Music	
25 Claverton Bdgs	⬜
Atrium Gallery	443446
4 The Podium, Northgate St.	🟡
Audience	333310
14 Broad St.	⬜

Retailers

Avon Film	460383	**Bath Sewing Machine Services**	460435
15 Argyle St.	⬜	76 Walcot St.	🟧
Avon Valley Cyclery	461880	**Bath Stamp and Coin**	463073
Rear of Bath Spa Station	🟦	12 Pulteney St.	🟧
Bang & Olufsen	**445211**	**Bath Sweet Shop**	
2 Argyle St.	⬜	Abbey Green	🟣
Bankes Books	444580	**Beaux Arts**	464850
5 Margaret's Buildings	🟡	12/13 York St.	🟠
Barrique	427423	**Bens Cookies**	460983
6 George St.	🟣	21 Union Passage	🟣
Bartlett Street Antique Centre	469998	**BI Too**	425308
Bartlett St.	🔴	34 Gay St.	🟨
Bath Antique Garden Centre	311106	**Big Sky Gallery**	**329800**
The Garden, 1 North Parade Bridge Rd.	🔴	**26 Broad St.**	🟠
Bath Aqua Theatre of Glass	428146	**Bijou Jewellery**	337822
Walcot St.	⚪	17 The Corridor	🟥
Bath Book Exchange	466214	**Bisque Radiators**	478508
35 Broad St.	🟡	23 Queen Square	⚪
Bath Compact Discs	464766	**Blacks Outdoor Specialists**	
11 Broad St.	⬜	High St.	🟦
Bath Deli, The	315666	**Bloomsbury**	461049
7 Margaret's Bdgs	🟣	15 New Bond St.	⚪
Bath Galleries	462946	**Bog Island News**	463874
33 Broad St.	🟠	North Parade	🟨
Bath Imaging Centre	333999	**Bonapartes**	
24 New Bond St.	⬜	13 George St.	🟦⚪
Bath Model Centre	460115	**Boots**	482069
2 Lower Borough Walls	🟦	25 Westgate St.	🟩
Bath Old Books	742755	**British Hatter, The**	339009
9c Margaret's Buildings	🔴🟡	9 Walcot St.	🟢
Bath Rugby Shop	311950	**Bus Station Flower Shop**	460121
1 Argyle St.	🟦	Manvers St.	🟧

130

Retailers

Camden Books	461606	**Duck Son & Pinker**	465975
146 Walcot St.	🟡	Pulteney Bridge	⬜
Cameron Cashmere	464592	**E.P. Mallory & Son Ltd.**	**465885**
19 Northumberland Place	🟢	**1-4 Bridge St.**	🟥
Card, The	465358	**Edgar Modern**	
5 Beau St.	🟪	Bartlett St.	🟠
Card Collection, The	**480122**	**Editor, The**	466474
11 The Podium	🟪	14 Kingsmead Square	🟨
Caroline Nevill Miniatures	443091	**Editor, The**	330818
22a Broad St.	○	The Tramshed, Walcot St.	🟨
Cat Out of the Bag	463868	**Editor, The**	427832
13 Northumberland Place	○	26 Westgate St.	🟨
Christopher Barry	464585	**Ellis & Killpartrick**	**466954**
Old Bond St.	🟢	**18 New Bond St.**	🟧
Coopers Electrical Superstore	311811	**E-Play**	444101
13-15 Walcot St.	⬜	3 Lower Borough Walls	⬜
Cornish Bakehouse	426635	**Eric Snooks's The Golden Cot**	464914
11a The Corridor	🟣	Abbey Gate St.	⬜
Crabtree & Evelyn	481519	**F.J. Harris & Son, Pictures**	462116
9 The Podium, Northgate St.	○	14 Green St.	🟠
Cudworth Artworks	445221	**Fast Signs**	447797
5 London St.	🟠	86 Walcot St.	🟧
Curtain Exchange, The	422078	**Fine Cheese Company, The**	483407
11 Widcombe Parade	⬜	29 Walcot St.	🟣
Definition	464396	**Fishworks**	447794
10 Broad St.	🟢	6 Green St.	🟣
Devon Savouries	442009	**FOPP**	
19 Lower Borough Walls	🟣	The Corridor	⬜
Dickinson, D & B Antiques	466502	**Framing Workshop, The**	482748
22 New Bond St.	🔴	128 Walcot St.	🟠
Dressing Room, The	330563	**Frederick Tranter**	466197
7 Quiet St.	🟢	5 Church St., Abbey Green	🟧

131

Retailers

Futon & Sofa Bed Shop, The	464052	**Habitat**	460623
27 Walcot St.	⚪	New Bond St.	⚪
Gap	463132	**Halfords**	445255
18-19 Old Bond St.	🟢	Westgate Buildings	🟧
Gear Change	442188	**Hampstead Bazaar**	789991
8 Claverton Buildings	🟢	4 Pulteney Bridge	🟢
General Trading Company, The	460907	**Han Classical Chinese Furniture**	424449
10 Argyle St.	○	29 Belvedere, Lansdown Rd.	🟠
George	**758100**	**Hansel und Gretel**	464677
19 Broad St.	⚪	4 Shires Yard, Milsom St.	○
George Bayntun	466000	**Hargreaves Sports**	461996
23 Manvers St.	🟠🟡	13 Westgate St.	🟦
Glass House	463436	**Hargreaves Sports**	462421
1 Orange Grove	○	9 The Mall	🟦
Gold & Silver Studio	462300	**Harington Glass**	482179
11a Queen St.	🟧	3 Queen St.	○
Good Buy Books	**469625**	**Harvest**	465519
6 North Parade	🟡	37 Walcot St.	🟣

Itchy Feet, Bartlett Street

Retailers

Hayes	465757	**John's Bikes**	334633
London St., Walcot	○	82 Walcot St.	■
Health and Beauty Centre	310014	**Just Add Water**	425644
11 Queen St.	■	The Corridor	■
High and Mighty	442143	**Just Rugby**	484998
1 Saracen St.	●	13 Northgate St.	■
Hot Bath News	423115	**K C Change**	448206
1 Hot Bath St.	■	13 Abbey Churchyard	○
House of Atmosphere	461028	**Karen Millen**	480516
24 Broad St.	○	10 New Bond St.	●
House of Bath	446266	**Kimberly**	466817
1-2 Bartlett St.	○	13 Trim St.	●
Husqvarna Viking Studio	482413	**Kirby & Garton**	469966
27 Charles St.	○	61 Walcot St.	○
Image	447359	**Kitchens**	330524
9 Shires Yard, Milsom St.	●	4 Quiet St.	○
Itchy Feet	337987	**Knob Connection, The**	465311
4 Bartlett St.	●	22 Broad St.	○
Jacaranda The Florist	442688	**Laura Ashley**	460341
9 Claverton Bdgs	■	New Bond St.	○
James Townsend Antiques	332290	**Leather Centre, The**	466528
1 Saville Row	●	12 Broad St.	●
Jaq Women	447975	**Leather Chairs of Bath**	447920
16 Margaret's Buildings	●	10a Bartlett St.	○
Jigsaw	461613	**Linen Press, The**	471683
8 New Bond St.	●	6 Margaret's Bdgs	○
JJB Sports	444755	**Lite Bite, The**	310099
23 High St.	■	6 London St.	●
Jo Christoforides		**Liz Cox**	445509
2 Sussex Place	■	17 Margaret's Bdgs	●
John Moore's Sports	466341	**London Road Stores**	336307
13 Argyle St.	■	London Rd.	■

Retailers

Lopburi	322947	**MasterShoe**	460509
5 Saville Row	🔴	92 Walcot St.	🟢
Lotus Emporium	**445500**	**MCCN Computer Solutions**	
19-20 The Corridor	🟧	128 Walcot St.	☐
Lotus Gallery	444480	**Mee**	442250
10 Chapel Row	🟠	9a Bartlett St.	🟢
M B's Tee Shirts	427514	**Mimi Yuyu**	**420333**
The Podium	🟢	**12 Margaret's Buildings**	🟧
M&K Hardware	339638	**Minerva Chocolate**	**464999**
Stall 32, Guildhall Market	⚪	**15 Abbey Church Yard**	🟣
Mailboxes Etc.	**483777**	**Minerva Graphics**	464054
3 Edgar Buildings, George St.	🟪	12a Trim St.	🟠
Mandarin Slate Ltd.	460033	**Mirror Shop, The**	
15-16 Broad St.	⚪	134 Walcot St.	⚪
Mangia Bene	336106	**Mondi**	444680
5/6 St James St.	🟣	Seven Dials, 5-6 Sawclose	🟢
Mary Rose Young	445899	**Moss of Bath**	331441
78 Walcot St.	⚪	45 St. James Parade	☐
		Multi Serve	462018
		7 Union Passage	🟧
		National Trust Shop, The	460249
		14 Abbey Churchyard	⚪
		Nauticalia	310531
		7 Pulteney Bridge	🟧
		News Plus	461734
		6 Argyle St.	🟨
		Nicholas Wylde	462826
		12 Northumberland Place	🟥
		No. 12 Queen Street	462363
		12 Queen St.	⚪
		Old Bank Antiques Centre	**469282**
		16-17 & 20 Walcot Bdgs	🔴

Ktwo's Six of the Best* Retailers

1. Rossiters
2. Waterstones
3. GAP
4. Square
5. Bloomsbury's
6. Kitchens

Retailers

On the Video Front	462033	**Red Eye**	465944
7 Terrace Walk	▫	28 Broad St.	🟢
Orbis Gifts	464001	**Replay Records**	444577
Abbey Green	○	26 Broad St.	▫
Orchard Arts	460805	**Rickards of Bath**	464107
Old Orchard, 88a Walcot St.	🟠	11 Northumberland Place	🟢
Oriental Rugs	**465558**	**Rohan**	462374
17 Argyle St.	⚪	16 Union Passage	🟦
Paddington and Friends	463598	**Rossiters of Bath**	462227
1 Abbey St.	○	38-41 Broad St.	🔵
Papyrus Stationery Emporium	463418	**Roundabout**	316696
8 Upper Borough Walls	🟪	2 Prior Park Rd	🟢
Paragon Antiques	463715	**Russell Rare Prints**	
3 Bladud Buildings, The Paragon	🔴	5 Margaret's Buildings	🟠
Paws for Thought	460514	**San Francisco Fudge Factory**	425714
12a Westgate St.	🟧	6 Church St.	🟣
Pax Marie	480660	**Sausage Shop, The**	318300
35 Walcot St.	⚪	7 Green St.	🟠
Paxton & Whitfield	466403	**ShakeAway**	466200
1 John St.	🟣	3 Beau St.	🟣
Print Room	447877	**Shannon**	424222
1 Sussex Pl.	🟠	68 Walcot St.	⚪
Pulteney Bridge Flowers	461938	**Shoon**	480095
14 Pulteney Bridge	🟧	14 Old Bond St.	🟢
Pulteney Bridge Toys & Gifts	426161	**Silver Shop, The**	464781
15-16 Pulteney Bridge	○	25 Union Passage	🟥
Quiet Street Antiques	315727	**Silvermine**	316382
3 Quiet St.	🔴	12 The Podium	🟥
Rachel James	471330	**Sixes and Sevens**	465124
12 Margaret's Buildings	🟢	8 Abbey Green	○
Reboot Computers	447227	**Smile Stores Ltd**	330747
106 Walcot St.	▫	James St. West, Green Park	🟨

Retailers

Somerfield	462868	**Trim Bridge Galleries**	466390
4 Marchants Passage	●	4 Trim Bridge	○
Somervale Antiques	412686	**TS2**	311266
6 Radstock Rd.	●	4 Upper Borough Walls	■
Spar News	464965	**Tumi**	446025
17 Broad St.	■	8 New Bond St.	○
Sportshoe	460509	**Utopia Jewellery**	**445524**
92 Walcot St.	●	**2 Abbey Green**	■
Springtide Gallery	425450	**Vintage Rare Guitars**	330888
13 Broad St.	○	7-8 Saville Row	●■
Square	334421	**Vom Fass**	**447660**
16 Northgate St.	●	**11A Shires Yard, Milsom St.**	●
Stitch	481134	**Waitrose**	442550
15 The Podium	■	The Podium, Northgate St.	●
Stone the Crows	460231	**Walcot Woollies**	463966
3 Broad St.	○	104 Walcot St.	●
Superdrug	421680	**Walters of Bath**	**446599**
30 Westgate St.	■	**16 The Podium**	□
Susan Gillis-Browne	463833	**Waterstones**	448515
5 Upper Borough Walls	●	4 Milsom St.	○
Sweet Shop, The	428040	**Westworld**	447006
8 North Parade Passage	●	36 Westgate St.	●
Test Office Products	444224	**Which Watch**	469299
18 Union Passage	■	7a Broad St.	□
Tog 24	335367	**White Company, The**	445284
6 Upper Borough Walls	●	15 Northgate St.	○
Toll House	312275	**Whiteman Bookshop**	464029
114-116 Walcot St.	○	6-7 Orange Grove	○
Total Fitness	444164	**Whittards of Chelsea**	428684
9 Saracen St.	■	10 Stall St.	●
Tridias	314730	**Widcombe Health Food Shop**	447980
124 Walcot St.	■	21 Claverton Bdgs	●

Retailers / Things To Do

Yellow Shop, The   404001
Walcot St.   🟢

Things To Do

For more info. visit www.finditbath.co.uk

THEATRES

The Rondo   448844
St Saviour's Rd., Larkhall
Theatre Royal   448831
Sawclose
Ustinov Studio Theatre   448831
Monmouth St.

CINEMAS

ABC   461730
Westgate St.
Little Theatre   466822
St Michael's Place

TOURS

Appointment with Fear   01904 700945
Ghost walk with costumed guide. From 8:10pm every night from Pump Room, Abbey Churchyard.
Bizarre Bath
Humourous look at Bath and its people, 8pm every evening in the summer outside The Huntsman pub, 1 Terrace Walk.
Ghost Walk   463618
Garricks Head pub near Theatre Royal, 8pm May-Oct & other times.
Great Bath Pub Crawl   310364
Sun-Wed throughout summer. 8pm at The Old Green Tree, Green St.
Mayors Honourary Guides
Give 2-hour free guided walks. 10:30am every day and other times from Abbey Churchyard.
Open Top Bus Tours
Choice of buses with live commentary and regular hop-on, hop-off services.

OTHER ACTIVITIES

Approach Golf Course   331162
18 & 12 hole pitch & putt.
Bath Balloon Flights   466888
Hot Air Balloon flights over Bath.
Bath City Boat Trips   07974 560197
Downstream from Pulteney Weir, full commentary, departures all day.
Bath Narrowboats   447276
Day boat hire. Sydney Wharf, Bathwick Hill.
Bath Racecourse   424609
Scheduled events throughout year.

Things To Do

Botanical Gardens and The Great Dell
Victoria Park

Entry Hill Golf Course 834248
Good nine holes.

Excel Tennis in the Park 425066
Royal Victoria Park

Heritage Balloons 318747
Hot Air Balloon flights over Bath.

Pleasure Boat Trips
From Pulteney Weir. Hourly in the summer (Easter - October).

Prior Park Landscape Garden
National Trust.

Thermae Bath Spa
Opening Soon. Hetling Pump Room, Hot Bath St.

Victoria Falls Adventure Golf 425066
Royal Victoria Park

Ktwo's Six of the Best* Things To Do

1. Canal Walk
2. Theatre Royal
3. Cinema
4. Walking
5. Walcot Flea Market
6. River Trip

NIGHT CLUBS

Cadillacs 464241
90 Walcot St

Fez 425677
The Paragon

Moles Club 404445
George St. Live music venue.

Po Na Na 401115
7-8 North Parade

CLUBS & SOCIETIES

Philosophy Group 312084
Bath Royal Literary & Scientific Institute, 16-18 Queen Square.
Speakers on a range of topics.

Bath & County Club 423732
Queens Prd. Bridge, yoga, book club.

SPORTS

Bath Rugby Club 325200
The Recreation Ground

Bath City Football Club 423087
Twerton Park

Bath Sports & Leisure Ctr 462565
North ParadeRd.

See a comprehensive list of 37 attractions in the Bath area on Find It Bath: www.finditbath.co.uk.

General Listing

General Listing

For more info. visit www.finditbath.co.uk

Emergency: Police, Fire, Ambulance
999 or 112

Police Station (incl lost property)
444343

Royal United Hospital (Accident and Emergency) **428331**

Bath Festival Booking Office
463362

Evening Chronicle 322322
Windsor House, Windsor Bridge

Main Post Office 0845 7223344
25 New Bond St.
Open: Mon to Sat, 9:00am - 5:30pm

Public Library 428144
The Podium, Northgate St.
Open: Mon, 10:00am - 6:00pm
Tue - Thu, 9:30am - 7:00pm
Fri - Sat, 9:30 - 5:00pm
Sun, 1:00pm - 4:00pm

Samaritans, 429222
2 New King St.

Ticketcall 447770
15 Pierrepont St.

Tickets & Bookings (TABS) 448831
Theatre Royal, Sawclose

Tourist Information Centre (TIC)
Abbey Church Yard 0906 711 2000
(50p/min)

The Assembly Rooms

Quizzes & Other Interesting Items

Booklet Quiz

You will find all the answers to this quiz within the pages of this guide booklet.

1. Where in Bath can one find a "Ha-Ha"?
2. Why is the post box on the corner of Cavendish Crescent unusual?
3. What did the Romans call the road we now know as Julian Road?
4. Name two things wrong with the "central" feature of Camden Crescent.
5. What are the three orders of architecture? (Here's a hint: visit the Circus)
6. How were the Assembly Rooms financed?
7. Where can one find extracts from the Magna Carta?
8. In The Kings Bath, what was the Kitchen?
9. Who presided over the coronation of King Edgar?
10. The design of Pulteney Bridge is said to be based on which Italian Bridge?

Kids Quiz

To help keep the kids busy and interested while walking through Bath.

1. How many doors are there in the Royal Crescent?
2. What do you think the Hot Spring Water tastes like?
3. What animal is above the doors in Lansdown Crescent?
4. Can you find the old horse trough/drinking fountain on Walcot Street?
5. Can you find any matching carvings above the doors and windows of the circus?
6. Using Roman numerals, what year was the Queen Square obelisk erected?
7. Do your hands fit into any of the Actors' hand prints in the Seven Dials fountain?
8. How many sheep are grazing on the Lansdown Crescent lawn?
9. How many angels on the ladders on the Abbey's west wall are facing head down?
10. Can you get to the centre of the Beazer Maze (by the river next, to the Recreation Ground).

City of Art & Festivals

Gorgon's Head Hunt

Find the nine hidden Gorgon's Heads within the photographs in this booklet and receive a prize! You'll have to look closely at the photographs in each chapter to find them. You can see the real thing of course at The Roman Baths Museum.

> For answers to the Booklet Quiz and for the details for the Gorgon's Head Hunt competition and prizes, please go to www.finditbath.co.uk

Bath - City of Festivals

Feb	Fashion
Feb-Mar	Literature
Mar	Shakespeare
Mar	Mid Somerset Music
May	Hot Air Balloon Fiesta
May-Jun	International Music
May-Jun	Fringe
Jun	Banjo
Jun	Somerset County Cricket
Jul	Boules
Jul-Aug	International Guitar
Aug	Bath Shakespeare
Sep	Kite
Sep	Jane Austen
Oct	Film
Nov	Mozart

Bath - A Magnet for Artists

The following actors, artists and writers have lived or stayed in Bath:

Jane Austen - *Sydney Place*
Thomas Barker - *Doric House*
William Beckford - *Lansdown Cres.*
Edmund Burke - *North Parade*
Thomas de Quincey - *Green Park*
Charles Dickens - *St. James's Square*
Thomas Gainsborough - *Circus*
Oliver Goldsmith - *North Parade*
Samuel Johnson - *Walcot Street*
Walter Savage Landor - *St. James's Square & Rivers Street*
Sir Thomas Lawrence - *Alfred Street*
Thomas Robert Malthus - *Portland Pl.*
Yehudi Menuhin - *Lansdown Grove Hotel*
Laurence Olivier - *Royal Cres. Hotel*
Sir Ralph Richardson - *Royal Cres. Hotel*
Sir Walter Scott - *South Parade*
Percy Bysshe Shelley - *Abbey Churchyard*
Richard Brinsley Sheridan - *New King Street*
Sarah Siddons - *The Paragon*
Tobias Smollett - *South Prd. & Gay St.*
Robert Southey - *Walcot Street*
William Makepeace Thackery - *Circus*
Josiah Wedgwood - *Westgate Buildings & Gay Street*
James Abbot McNeill Whistler - *Marlborough Street*
William Wordsworth - *North Parade*

MAP of the CITY of BATH

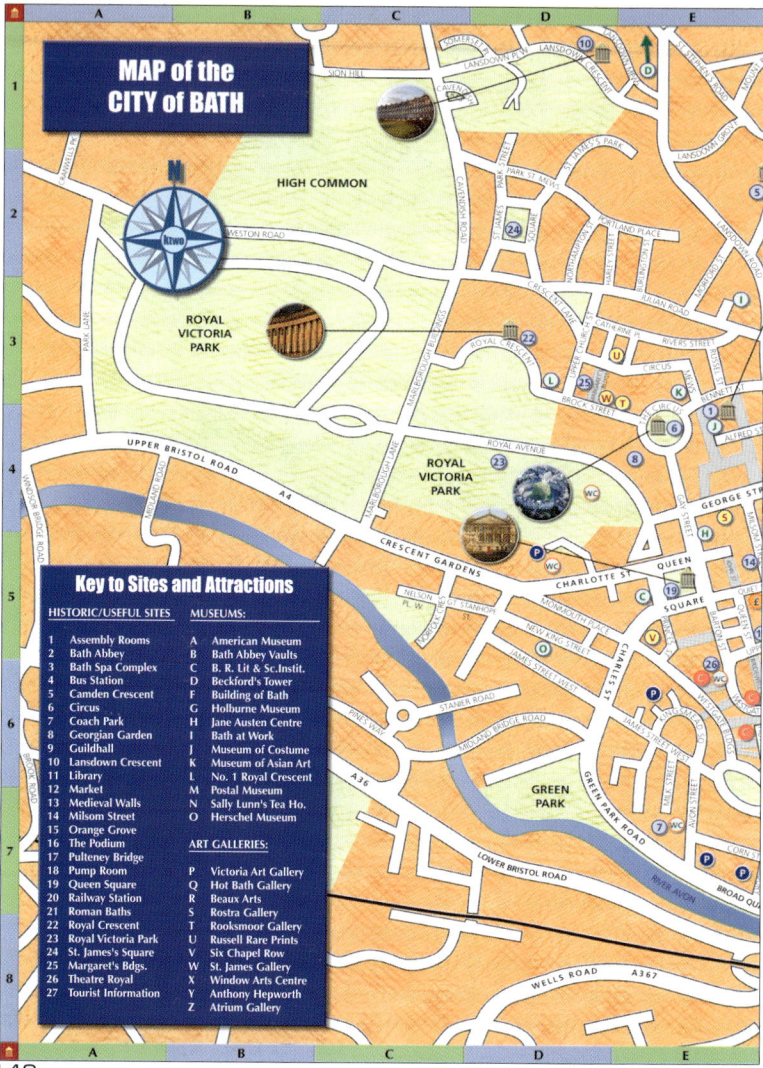

Key to Sites and Attractions

HISTORIC/USEFUL SITES

1. Assembly Rooms
2. Bath Abbey
3. Bath Spa Complex
4. Bus Station
5. Camden Crescent
6. Circus
7. Coach Park
8. Georgian Garden
9. Guildhall
10. Lansdown Crescent
11. Library
12. Market
13. Medieval Walls
14. Milsom Street
15. Orange Grove
16. The Podium
17. Pulteney Bridge
18. Pump Room
19. Queen Square
20. Railway Station
21. Roman Baths
22. Royal Crescent
23. Royal Victoria Park
24. St. James's Square
25. Margaret's Bdgs.
26. Theatre Royal
27. Tourist Information

MUSEUMS:

A. American Museum
B. Bath Abbey Vaults
C. B. R. Lit & Sc.Instit.
D. Beckford's Tower
F. Building of Bath
G. Holburne Museum
H. Jane Austen Centre
I. Bath at Work
J. Museum of Costume
K. Museum of Asian Art
L. No. 1 Royal Crescent
M. Postal Museum
N. Sally Lunn's Tea Ho.
O. Herschel Museum

ART GALLERIES:

P. Victoria Art Gallery
Q. Hot Bath Gallery
R. Beaux Arts
S. Rostra Gallery
T. Rooksmoor Gallery
U. Russell Rare Prints
V. Six Chapel Row
W. St. James Gallery
X. Window Arts Centre
Y. Anthony Hepworth
Z. Atrium Gallery

143

Thank you to the following for their help and kind support:

Grahame & Linda Baker-Smith
Pat Dunlop
Andy Forster
Jesse Loughborough
Jo Menneer
Jack Owen
Jill Reeves
Jeremy Seal
Niko Troupe

Published by Ktwo, Belgrave Lodge, Upper Camden Place, Bath BA1 5JA
Telephone: 0800 652 8245 Website: www.finditbath.co.uk